YS OF

JL

PEROWNE

YORK · SYDNEY · TORONTO

Published by the Hamlyn Publishing Group Limited
London · New York · Sydney · Toronto
Hamlyn House, 42 The Centre, Feltham, Middlesex, England

© Copyright the Hamlyn Publishing Group Limited 1973

ISBN 0 600 35214 5

Printed in Spain by Printer, Industria Gráfica S.A.
Tuset 19, Barcelona, San Vicente dels Horts 1972.
Depósito Legal B. 44572-1972. Mohn Gordon Ltd. London

CONTENTS

To

GEOFFREY WOODHEAD

Fellow of Corpus Christi College, Cambridge

Old Pauline and Governor of Saint Paul's School

'Nam quaecunque homines bene cuiquam dicere possunt

Aut facere, haec a te dictaque factaque sunt.'

COLOUR PLATES

CHAPTER ONE

STEPHEN, AND SAUL OF TARSUS

Pontius Pilate had been governor of Judaea for ten years, from AD 27 to 36, and now at last he was gone. No one knew why the emperor Tiberius had kept him there so long. When people enquired, Tiberius would only quote Aesop's fable of the fox and the flies. The fox declined the offer of a friendly hedgehog to brush away the flies from his wounds, on the ground that the flies who were there had had a good meal, whereas newcomers would start all over again. Officials were the same, said the emperor. The truth was that Tiberius, now seventy-seven, after a bitter and frustrated life, had practically abdicated. In fact he was no longer even in Rome, but in well-guarded seclusion on the island of Capri. No wonder the administration of the empire had suffered, and nowhere more than in the highly sensitive province of Judaea which, because of its geographical position between Egypt and Syria and its proximity to Parthia, was of the first importance to Rome.

Politically, that is; in the eyes of its inhabitants it was no mere frontier bastion but the holiest place on earth. Few Romans understood who the Jews were, and what they stood for. When in 63 BC Pompey the Great occupied Palestine, he gave unforgivable offence to the Jewish people by profaning the Temple of the One and Only, Most High God. (Cicero thought Pompey had done splendidly—'our Jerusalemite' he called him.) Among the few men of discernment was Julius Caesar. He realized that the Jews were morally superior to others, more trustworthy, and therefore to be treated with respect and equity. As a result of their integrity, and aided by the political malaise endemic in their homeland once the Gentiles had possessed it, the Jews had spread amazingly throughout the empire. By the time of Augustus they must have numbered 4,500,000 if not more, that is seven per cent of the total population of the empire. But all of them looked to Jerusalem as their mother city.

Ever since Pompey's day, a headlong collision with Rome had seemed inevitable; but it had been averted or rather deferred by two men, father and son, who though Jews by religion were Idumeans, Arabs from southern Palestine. The first was Antipater, the second Herod the Great. Antipater had been granted hereditary Roman citizenship by Caesar, and Herod became the personal friend of Augustus and of his great minister Agrippa.

During Herod's lifetime, strict and at times cruel though he often was, Judaea had peace. God was praised in Zion, and the Holy City itself was embellished with two magnificent palaces, a new water-supply, a hippodrome and other amenities. Above all, Herod completely rebuilt the Temple, enlarging the enclosure on which it stood to no less than thirty-five acres. The Holy House itself glittered with costly marbles and golden tiles. Jerusalem had indeed become what a Roman encyclopaedist, Pliny the Elder, was soon to call it, 'the most splendid city not only of Judaea but of the whole Levant'.

When Herod died, after a reign of thirty-three years, the political fabric fell to pieces. Ravaged, in his last years, by bodily and mental decay he had killed three of his sons, his wife, her mother and others of his relations, so that there was no sure succession. The realm was fragmented by its

A narrow street in the old quarter of Jerusalem, believed to be the Via Dolorosa—the way from the Antonia fortress to the little knoll without the city wall along which Jesus stumbled under the weight of the baulk of timber which formed the horizontal beam of the cross on which he was to die.

Jerusalem, a view from the Mount of Olives. Jesus would have seen the city from, or near this point when returning from Bethany, and on the occasion in *Luke* XIX. 19, when he wept over it, knowing what was to come. The Temple occupied the site where the Dome of the Rock, one of Islam's holy places, now stands. Above and just to the right of the Dome can be seen the Lutheran church tower which stands just outside the walls of the New Testament city; close by are the Church of the Holy Sepulchre and the place identified as Golgotha, where Jesus was crucified.

Roman suzerain, Augustus, the new ruler being a son of Herod and a Samaritan mother called Archelaus. He was brought up largely in Rome; and thus to the Jews he was doubly alien. After a decade of inadequate and fretful charade, Archelaus was banished, and Augustus would have no more cardboard kings: the country must become a province, and one of the third rank, like Corsica, or Sardinia, with neither a legate nor a proconsul to rule it, but a mere procurator. Thus again did Rome humiliate the Jews and thus, inevitably, was a yeasty nationalism fostered. The Zealots were born—the very sect, *Qanna'im* in Hebrew, who were to be responsible for the destruction of the Temple in AD 70. (This charge is made by Josephus, the Jewish historian, but it is supported by the only mention of the Zealots in the Talmud (*Aboth* of Rabbi Nathan VI), who says that when Vespasian came to destroy Jerusalem, the *Qanna'im* attempted to burn everything with fire.) As so often in later times, terrorism was beginning to lead a nation to destroy itself.

Rome without, dissension within. So things had gone on until the days of the fifth procurator,

Below:
Events in Judaea in New Testament times were directly influenced by the power of Rome. Pompey *(left)* occupied Palestine in 63 BC and profaned the Temple in Jerusalem – a bad beginning to a Roman-Jewish relationship which was never better than uneasy. At its best it saw the approval of Augustus and Agrippa for the firm administration of Herod the Great. Herod's admiration for Agrippa *(centre)* caused both his grandson *(Acts* XIII) and his great-grandson *(Acts* XXV) to be named after him. The imperial throne was occupied by Tiberius *(right)* during the events related in the Gospels.

Pilate. From the outset of his term, he had shewn himself to be tactless, cruel, and weak. Jerusalem was not even the capital any more: the alien governor ruled from the new city of Caesarea, Herod's largely pagan creation on the coast. Now, as men looked at the Temple, still the great national rallying-point, and then at the arrogant cohorts who came to maintain 'security' during their holy festivals, they might have wondered whether the great days could ever return. And if so, how? Must they, the Chosen People of God, for ever be the bondservants of Rome?

Into this great debate a most disturbing factor had recently been introduced. There was a body of Jews, mostly from Jerusalem and Galilee, who declared that a certain Jesus—the one whom Pilate had so nearly let off when he was arraigned for blasphemy—was none other than the Messiah, the Anointed One, who was to restore the glory of Israel, and that he had proclaimed that all men, not only Jews, were entitled to be citizens of the Kingdom of Heaven. This idea outraged almost everyone, because it was anti-Roman and anti-orthodox; especially the Pharisees, who believed passionately in being separate, which is what the word Pharisee means. Nevertheless, this novel view of human destiny (for that is what the new movement was) attracted an alarming number of upright and godly men and women.

There were at this time two main parties in the Jewish polity. The ruling establishment were the Sadducees, hard-headed and hard-hearted materialists, who had for some time monopolized the High Priesthood, and the very considerable perquisites which went with it. On the other side were the Pharisees, themselves divided into two schools; the disciples of Shammai, an extreme rigorist, and the liberal followers of the saintly and famous Hillel, who had successfully advocated non-violence in the troubles that followed on Archelaus' banishment. In this new crisis, many, as was to be expected, including the Shammai Pharisees, wanted the dissidents suppressed by force. Others counselled caution, and finally the question was taken to Gamaliel. Gamaliel was the grandson of Hillel, and the greatest doctor of the day, acknowledged as *Rabban*, master, by all. The Mishnah has preserved several of his legal dicta, delivered on the steps of the Temple. 'With his death,' says the tractate *Sota*, IX. 16. 'the glory of the Law was extinguished, and with it perished purity and Pharisaism.'

Peter and the other apostles were rounded up and brought before the Sanhedrin, the Supreme Court of Jewry. The majority were clearly for a drastic sentence. Gamaliel moved that the court sit in camera, and then gave it as his opinion that if the new Way was false it would fail, as so many other movements had, and he cited recent examples. If on the other hand it was of God, to oppose it would be 'fighting against God'. Better let it take its course.

One of Gamaliel's pupils, who had sat at his feet as the master taught on the sacred steps, reacted violently to the great man's decision. His name was Saul, and he came from Tarsus, a city in Asia Minor, on the Cydnus, the river up which Cleopatra had sailed to captivate Mark Antony in 41 BC: Shakespeare has made it immortal—

> The barge she sat in, like a burnish'd throne,
> Burn'd on the water: the poop was beaten gold;
> Purple the sails, and so perfumed that
> The winds were love-sick with them; the oars
>   were silver,
> Which to the tune of flutes kept stroke and made
> The water which they beat to follow faster,
> As amorous of their strokes. For her own person,
> It beggar'd all description: she did lie
> In her pavilion, cloth-of-gold of tissue,
> O'er picturing that Venus where we see
> The fancy outwork nature: on each side of her
> Stood pretty dimpled boys, like smiling Cupids,
> With divers-coloured fans, whose wind did
>   seem
> To glow the delicate cheeks which they did cool,
> And what they undid did.

Shakespeare is here paraphrasing Plutarch, who wrote his description some hundred and fifty years later; yet so vivid are the details in his narrative it is clear that the scene must have made a deep and abiding impression on those who witnessed it. Saul's father may well have been among them. Perhaps it was on this occasion that the family acquired Roman citizenship, or it could have been a few years earlier when Cicero was governor of Cilicia, of which Tarsus was the capital. The later date seems the more probable, because although Paul was proud of being a Roman citizen, and says so emphatically on several occasions, he never mentions his *gens* or clan. The Herods, who were Julians, constantly do. If Saul was of Antony's *gens*, his silence is understandable, because Augustus, after his defeat of Antony and Cleopatra at Actium in 31 BC and their subsequent suicides, had ordered Antony's statues to be overthrown and his name blotted from the records.

The modern term Asia Minor is misleading. In

antiquity it was not *minor* in any sense of the word: it was very major. The geographical setting is majestic; lofty mountains, often snow-capped, rising to the heavens, with wide, fertile plains at their feet, watered by great and bountiful rivers, one of which, the Meander, from the sinuosities of its fruitful course, has added a word to the English language.

This inscription, probably carved on the base of a dedicatory statue, comes from the Roman theatre at Caesarea, the capital of the Roman province of Judaea. It is of great importance because it shows clearly the names of the emperor Tiberius (in adjectival form) and Pontius Pilate, the donor. The first three letters of *Pontius* are missing but the identification is beyond doubt. It is the only pagan Latin reference to Pontius Pilate except for the famous sentence in Tacitus (*Annals* xv. 44,4), written nearly a hundred years later.

Great cities, of which Tarsus was one, arose in this generous country: Ephesus, Pergamum, Perga, Priene (whose grid town-plan has been the model for many another throughout the world). And it was here, in Ionia, that philosophy had its birth, long before it illuminated Athens, here that men first discarded myth, and asked 'What is truth?'.

Though technically Hellenistic Tarsus was, as Pliny reminds us, more Phoenician than Greek. It was a busy trading centre like other Phoenician cities such as Tyre and Sidon. Its citizens travelled far and wide: one, a grammarian called Demetrius, even went as far as Britain, as we know from Plutarch. So Paul, who never visited Britain, may well have heard of it from his father, who was a contemporary of the enterprising Demetrius.

In a later age, after the Faith which Paul preached had been established in Britain by St Augustine of Canterbury in 597, Tarsus did make a direct contribution to this country. In the year 669 Theodore of Tarsus became the first Primate of All England. Four years later he summoned a synod at Hertford, which antedated parliament in England by more than a century. The Venerable Bede describes it in great detail.

Side by side with the lucrative textile trade philosophy still flourished in Tarsus, especially that of the Stoics—Augustus himself had been a pupil of a Tarsian Stoic. Chrysippus, the man who was held to be the second founder of Stoicism, went from Cilicia to hold the chair at Athens from 232 to 207 BC. In the following century two of the *Prostatai*, as they were called, were from Tarsus; Zeno, who succeeded in 204 and Antipater, from about 150 to 129. Tarsus was a Stoic stronghold.

That Paul was much influenced by the Stoics is clear from his writings. This is of particular interest, because the founder of Stoicism was not a Greek but like Saul a Semite, Zeno of Kitium in Cyprus. Paul was brought up as a strict Jew, a Pharisee; but his vernacular was Hellenistic Greek and it was in the standard Greek version, made in Alexandria in 284–287 BC and known as the Septuagint, that Saul studied his scriptures.

He also studied mankind. Like Socrates before him, Saul was little interested in nature; they were both city-dwellers. Saul was apprenticed to the family business, a textile industry which specialized in the manufacture of a tough goat-hair fabric used in the making of tents. He knew all about the sports of the city; the running, the wrestling, the boxing, even if he did not take part in them, as many pious Jews did not, because they held sinful the nudity in which they were conducted.

'Tarsus to-day,' says Professor Seton Lloyd, 'is a rather unattractive little Turkish town on the mainroad from Adana to Mersin. Its only monument is a ruined gateway which the American missionaries used to call "Paul's Arch", though it is in fact Byzantine in date. As for the great lake, the town is now separated from the sea by about ten miles of uninhabited marshes.' But Tarsus being dead, yet speaketh by the mouth of its greatest citizen. A proud Pharisee, a proud speaker of Greek, a proud Roman citizen, of about thirty years of age—such was the Saul who who now intervened in the critical affairs of Jerusalem Jewry.

The tolerant wisdom of his teacher (who was known to favour things Greek) was alien to this fiery Cilician, and he took another course. Among the adherents of the new way—which already to Saul's chagrin included two of his relations—was an outstanding young man called Stephen, of remarkable beauty and great ability. He was one of seven 'deacons', or servants, recently appointed to look after the human wants of the aged, specially the widows who were not Jewish by birth. (It is well to recall that in its very infancy, as in later centuries, the Church had a concern, to use a good Quaker word, for the care of the underprivileged.) Stephen worked wonders, people said.

His success roused Saul's associates to action. His synagogue—one of many which now existed in Jerusalem—was that of Hellenized Jews from Egypt and Asia Minor who found the locals, few of whom could speak Greek, backward and dull. It was for Saul and his associates to take the initiative—and to take it quickly. Saul, being a Roman citizen, from a well-governed province, knew that no Roman governor would countenance lynch law, and that if he and his friends were going to take action they must do so at once, during the interregnum between Pilate's departure and the arrival of his successor.

Stephen was charged with being blasphemous and a subverter of the establishment, and arraigned before the Sanhedrin. He made a brilliant defence, so brilliant that many in the court considered that he not only looked like an angel but spoke like one. The verdict, nevertheless, was inevitable. Strictly speaking, the Jewish religious court, as in the case of Jesus of Nazareth, could only find a man *worthy* of death; the *order* for execution must come from the Roman governor. There being no governor at the time, Saul and his friends could dispense with formality. They dragged Stephen out of the city to a little hill just to the east of the great north road, and there stoned him to death, that being the prescribed penalty for blasphemy. The director of operations was Saul himself: it was in his care that the stoning-party left their outer cloaks, so that their arms should be unencumbered.

The successful stoning of Stephen greatly encouraged the orthodox: they started a purge, on a

Jesus before Pilate, a detail from the great panel, the *Maestà* (majesty), painted by Duccio di Buoninsegna for the cathedral of Siena in the early fourteenth century. Pontius Pilate was not loved by either Jews or Romans but he held the office of procurator for more than ten years—which explains why he had grown tired and timid when he had to preside over the trial of Jesus.

house-to-house inquisition in which Saul took the lead. The followers of the 'way' were scattered; only the apostles stayed on in Jerusalem. Saul received congratulations from all quarters—except one: his conscience. Stoning is a slow, brutal death, and Saul had been forced to observe how Stephen bore it. It was with absolute constancy. He died with a prayer of forgiveness on his smashed and shapeless lips.

During later persecutions of the Church, we have abundant evidence that it was the bearing of the martyrs that was the most effective argument in favour of the Faith. So it was with Saul. He would have denied it vehemently: men commonly deny that which they believe most ardently. Peter had set a precedent for it. Saul, who was to become

Above, left:
St Stephen's Gate in Jerusalem. This is not as might be supposed near the place where the first Christian martyr met his death. The stoning took place near the Damascus Gate *(right)* in the north wall and a martyr's shrine was built there in the fifth century AD. The structure of both gates as seen today date from the time of Suleiman the Magnificent.

his fellow-worker, was unconsciously following that precedent. 'The kingdom of heaven,' says the shortest parable in the New Testament, 'is like unto leaven, which a woman took, and hid in three measures of meal, till the whole was leavened.'

Already the leaven was at work, already Saul the slayer was, by the grace of God, being transformed into Paul the apostle.

The stoning of Stephen, a detail from one of the tapestries designed by Raphael for the Sistine Chapel and now in the Pinacoteca Vaticana. The young man in the foreground seated by the heap of clothing is Saul of Tarsus, who supervised this murder. Stoning was slow and protracted – the victim suffered unspeakably. Saul was to see how courageously Stephen, firm in his faith, met his death.

CHAPTER TWO

CONVERSION AND CALL

The persecution was going well. How wrong Gamaliel had been, and how right Saul of Tarsus, must now be clear to all. It really had not been so hard; the main thing had been to make an example of one of the ringleaders and that had been done. Stephen had been put to death and the rest had scattered, all except the hard core of the innovators who had stayed on in Jerusalem. And what did a dozen peasants from Galilee matter, one way or the other?

Then came some rather disturbing news. The followers of the Way as they would call it, instead of going underground like sensible folk, were actively spreading their propaganda. Strange tales came from Samaria, fifty miles north of Jerusalem. Admittedly it was a pagan town, the creation of Herod the Great, but it was uncomfortably near the Holy City. Besides it was not pleasant to hear that one of the Galileans had actually got the better of a local magician, with the result that a flourishing 'cell' had been founded in Samaria, visited by two of the apostles themselves, who on their way back to Jerusalem had spread their ideas in a number of villages. The same thing had been happening in the south. One of these men—it was the same one, called Philip, who had started the Samaria branch—had actually won over a foreign diplomatist, an envoy from the Ethiopian court. Finally there came news that even in Damascus, that famous and ancient city, these new theories were gaining ground. Saul was perturbed: it was not going to be quite as easy as it had seemed to stamp out this new cult.

Saul found the high priest, Theophilus son of Annas, sympathetic. By all means let Saul go to Damascus, and bring back the dissidents under arrest, even if they were women, to be dealt with by the Sanhedrin. Whether this was legal or not did not matter. Damascus, although it was one of the Decapolis, the Ten Cities (there were really eleven), or Greek colonies in the Levant, had been leased by Caligula, Tiberius' successor, to Harith (Aretas) IV, king of the Nabateans, from the year AD 37 for three years. Tiberius had been on bad terms with Harith, and Caligula was anxious to make it up, because the Nabatean kingdom marched with the ever-menacing Parthians. The king in his turn was willing to collaborate with the Jewish hierarchy.

Saul set off. As he rode out of the northern gate of Jerusalem he passed the spot on which he had Stephen put to death but a short while before. Saul and his companions pressed on up the great trunk road. Their route would take them past Samaria, and the fringe of Galilee, down into the Jordan valley, where they would cross the river. The journey thus far would have occupied the best part of a week. The hardest trek was yet to come, the long grind up from the Sea of Galilee seven hundred feet below the level of the Mediterranean, to Damascus, more than two thousand feet above it. He still had fifty miles to go, over the bleak, steep way. He had plenty of time for thought, about the past, about the future, and the task that lay before him. At last, the lovely oasis, the shining city, 'the diamond set in an emerald' as it was to be called, came in sight, with the snow-crowned peak of Mount Hermon above it. Saul should have felt at peace again—yet he could not have been at peace. And suddenly he gave way.

The experience of Saul before the gate of

Facing:
The conversion. Caravaggio's remarkable painting, *The Conversion of St Paul*, emphasizes 'a light from heaven' and shows Saul, fallen from his horse lying on the ground blinded with shock.

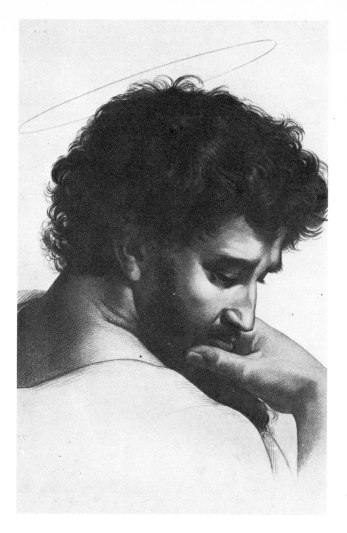

Damascus is one of the most dramatic in the history of man, and one of the most pregnant, because the fruit of it changed the history of the world.

What *did* happen?

To be able to understand at least partially what happened, we must separate the *phenomenon* from the *experience*. Because the phenomenon seemed to be so awful, so mysterious, it is better known than the experience, if only because so many painters and hymn-writers have attempted to portray it. Awful it was, but not mysterious. There are three accounts in *Acts* of it, all substantially the same, two by Saul himself. 'At midday . . . I saw in the way a light from heaven, above the brightness of the sun, shining round about me and them which journeyed with me' (XXVI. 13). 'And I fell unto the ground, and heard a voice saying unto me, Saul, Saul, why persecutest thou me? And I answered, Who art thou, Lord? And he said unto me, I am Jesus of Nazareth, whom thou persecutest. And they that were with me saw indeed the light, and were afraid; but they heard not the voice of him that spoke to me.' (XXII. 7–9). Paul is addressing the throng in the Temple precinct. He

Paul has been a popular subject with the great painters. Rubens saw him as a traditional, patriarch-like figure *(above, left)* while Raphael's portrait *(above, right)*, from his *Saint Cecilia*, reflects the Italian faces he saw around him. The evidence, such as it is, suggests that Paul was much more like the distinctly Levantine figure who appears in the mosaic roundel in the sixth-century Arian Baptistery at Ravenna *(facing page)*. See the description of him on page 42.

repeats the account in XXVI, when addressing Agrippa II, adding (to conciliate the Jewish king) that the voice spoke to him in Hebrew, and also said: 'It is hard for thee to kick against the pricks', a proverbial saying as old as Pindar.

Is this myth, or miracle, or 'exteriorization' of inner conflict? It is none of them. It is a simple, natural phenomenon. Exactly the same thing happened in Jerusalem some fifteen years ago. It was on Christmas Day, again about noon. After matins, a number of friends had gathered in an upper room of the American Colony, which is only a hundred yards from the cathedral of St George. One of the guests was standing at the window, looking across to the church. Without

Mount Hermon crowned with snow, another landmark on the fateful journey. Lying to the north of the road to Damascus it would have been visible throughout the long climb on horseback – Damascus is 2,264 feet high.

Right:
The long gap in our knowledge of Paul's life immediately after his conversion may never be filled. Such facts as we have tells us that he was in Arabia – that is, the kingdom of the Nabateans – for some of the time. The capital was the famous 'rose-red' Petra then, as now, almost inaccessible. The massive rock walls of the Siq dwarf the horseman threading through the two-mile defile which is the only way to the city.

Facing page:
The lake on the course of the River Jordan known as the Sea of Galilee where the river resumes its southward course. Saul and his companions passed this way and had to ascend 655 feet before reaching true sea level.

any warning, from a blue sky, there came a blinding flash of lightning, which seemed to obliterate the sun, accompanied (not followed, it was so close) by a terrifying clap of thunder. Being certain that the lightning must have hit the cathedral, the witness at once went back to St George's, to find that the lightning had indeed struck the building, had shattered one of the pinnacles of the tower, had damaged the bishop's house, inside which it had thrown a man to the ground. That is precisely how the incident appears in the recollection of one who observed it at very close quarters, and as in all such cases, it is the recollection which matters.

This is just what had happened to Saul and his companions nearly two thousand years before, and that is how they, too, recollected it. Only to them it was more terrifying. Thunder and lightning, of which the origin was unknown, were not only a frightening manifestation of divine power in an age which did not distinguish the natural from the supernatural, but also, in the pre-explosive age, the loudest noise, and the brightest light known to man. And they came from heaven. As for the voice, a voice was the *normal* method of learning of the divine will. Adam heard a voice, Isaiah heard a voice, Sokrates heard a voice, Saint Augustine heard a voice, Joan of Arc heard several; and Bunyan heard one '. . . that would sound so loud within me, yea, and as it were call so strongly after me, that once, above all the rest, I turned my head over my shoulder, thinking verily that some man had, behind me, called me'. *(Grace Abounding.)*

So much for the phenomenon. It was natural and normal. But the experience? That was a secret that Saul was to spend the rest of his life trying to analyse and to expound. He knew now that he had won the freedom for which God had reserved him from his mother's womb, that on the brink of utter disaster—he had been persecuting God, not men—he had been hauled back to safety, salvation, by the hand of a forgiving God. St Augustine once said, in his *Confessions*, 'The more wretched I became, the nearer You became.' That is what had happened to Saul. It has happened to many others since. Saul was given the grace to see it—in a flash.

We now come to the most tantalizing period in

Paul's journey to Damascus, where he intended to further his persecution of the followers of the new Way, would have led him through country like this, little changed since New Testament times. The hills of Samaria are seen in the distance and in the foreground the ruined walls of the Roman city of Sebaste. Paul would have travelled on a road going north and skirting Samaria on the east.

Above:
On his first journey Paul was the companion of Barnabas, a Cypriot Jew. The first call was in fact in Cyprus, at Salamis, and it is there that the memory of Barnabas is particularly honoured. The picture shows the Monastery of St Barnabas.

Left:
The eastern shore of the Dead Sea under winter clouds. Paul would have passed this way going from Damascus to Petra. He would also have passed through Jerash *(left, below)*, the ruins of which indicate that this, one of the many cities of the region, was a flourishing centre of considerable beauty.

Below:
The ruins of Perge, with those of the older, upper city in the background. The setting was typical of the cities of Hellenistic Asia visited by Paul during his first missionary journey. Perge was to become the centre of the Christian church in the province of Pamphylia.

Paul's life (let us begin to use his apostolic name). He had heard the Voice, but for all but himself it was almost literally *vox et praeterea nihil*—for seventeen whole years. We learn from *Acts* that Paul, still in a state of shock from his experience, was 'led by the hand' into the city and taken to lodge with a certain Judas, perhaps an innkeeper, in the street called Straight. It is still called that, in Arabic, and it is still a main artery. Vestiges of its sumptuous double colonnade still remain. Paul continued without food or drink for three days— Luke the physician, who gives us this information, would not overlook this physiological detail. Paul had been told by the Voice that he was to enter Damascus and that it would be told him what he must do. He now received a visit from a follower of the new faith, called Ananias, the traditional site of whose house, now a shrine, is just north of the street called Straight, at its eastern end.

When first Ananias had received his admonition (again, it was by a Voice), he had objected that 'Saul of Tarsus' was a well-known persecutor of the faithful. The Voice replied that Saul was to be 'a chosen vessel', to take the Name before the Gentiles and kings and the children of Israel. Ananias did as he was commanded, went to see Paul, and laid his hands on him, saying that he had been sent by the same Jesus whom Saul had seen on his journey. At once 'the scales fell from his eyes', he got up and was baptized. He then had a meal and felt better. (Here again the doctor speaks.) In his surviving writings Paul mentioned baptism nine or ten times, but he never refers to his own. It marks the crossing over a line from death to life which he had already passed.

Now comes the blank period, only illuminated by a few lines in Paul's letter to the Galatians, written twenty years later.

'I went into Arabia,' he says, 'and then returned again unto Damascus. Then after three years I went up to Jerusalem to see Peter, and abode with him fifteen days. But other of the apostles saw I none save James the Lord's brother. . . . Afterwards I came into the regions of Syria and Cilicia. . . . Then fourteen years after I went up again to Jerusalem with Barnabas. . . .'

Seventeen years! Seventeen years is a long period in any man's life, but these seventeen years in this man's life—how tantalizing is our ignorance.

Damascus, 'the street which is called Straight'. The ancient capital of Syria, Damascus is mentioned in written history as long ago as the sixteenth century BC. This very street has existed for as long as the city and still bears the same name; it is a main artery running from east to west.

Right:
The aqueduct at Antioch in Pisidia. Paul and Barnabas journeyed on foot from the coast at Perge to the plateau, 3,000 feet high, to reach the little town and its Jewish community.

Below:
The Temple of Nike on the Acropolis, with the modern city of Athens in the distance. Athens, one of the few places where Paul met with apparent total failure, was in his time only a shadow of the city of Perikles. But it still exercised a great attraction as a centre of learning and much of its beauty could still be discerned.

Facing page:
The Isthmus of Corinth, looking north from Acrocorinth. The Isthmus road led on to Athens by way of Eleusis.

Tarsus was a city in the Roman province of Cilicia, and a flourishing one–'no mean city', as Paul described it. When Roman power declined it was captured and recaptured by the armies of Islam and Byzantium and eventually the silt from the high ground, formerly no threat since the land was intensely cultivated, choked the harbour on the Cydnus river. There is little to be seen now of the city's former glory.

Right:
Petra, the rock-hewn city of the Nabateans, is not mentioned by name in the New Testament but there is a strong suggestion that Paul visited there when he 'went into Arabia'.

Facing page:
Detail of a twelfth-century mosaic in the Palatine Chapel of Roger II in Palermo. Paul is seen, left, disputing with the Damascenes and, right, making his escape in a basket let down by a rope from the city walls. This is the incident referred to in Paul's second letter to the Corinthians, where the man he fears is 'the governor under Aretas the King'. This supplements *Acts* IX, where it is the Jews of Damascus who 'took counsel to kill him'. King and Jews were temporarily at least, allies (p. 000).

But let us summarize what little we do know. First, Paul goes off to Arabia, which in this context means the kingdom of the Nabateans. What did he do there? No one knows. Some have conjectured that he went to some desert community, such as the Essenes of Qumran, for a brief retreat. Ricciotti gives him only 'a few months'. Bornkamm, on the other hand says he was in Arabia for two and a half to three years, but not years spent in monastic solitude and meditation. 'This edifying but fanciful picture modelled on the anchorites of the early church finds no support in the letters, and is at odds with his clear and express commission to preach.'

He would have visited the flourishing cities of Jerash, Philadelphia (Amman) and Petra, the capital of king Harith (Aretas), whom Paul mentions in *2 Corinthians* XI. 32. To those who know

the topography there is another slight but significant hint that Paul did visit Petra. In this same letter to the *Galatians* (IV. 24), speaking of Agar (Hagar), he throws in the gratuitous aside, 'For this Agar is Mount Sinai in Arabia'. Hagar in Hebrew is the same as Petra in Greek, and means 'rock'—from which most of Petra is hewn. To this day it is known as the Valley of Moses in Arabic, and the hill opposite is called Mount

Aaron, and is accounted holy. The mountain now known as Sinai can only be said to be 'in Arabia' by a very wide stretch and was at the time of the Exodus an Egyptian military post, the last place the fleeing Israelites would be likely to visit. Some scholars therefore do equate Petra with Sinai. Paul may well have done the same, from personal knowledge.

If Paul did preach in these cities, he had no great

33

success. He would have aroused opposition, which forced him to go back to Damascus. In that city, too, an official of the Nabatean king plotted against him, and Paul was compelled to flee, being let down over the wall in a basket. It is only then, two or three years after his conversion, that he goes up to Jerusalem to see Peter. This was really little more than a courtesy visit—courtesy all the more becoming in one who had but three short years ago been the chief enemy of Peter and his flock. As Bornkamm tartly puts it: 'The mention of his short visit to Cephas',—it was only a fortnight, remember—'comes under the rubric "for I did not receive my gospel from man, nor was I taught it". (*Galatians* I. 12.) A late catechumenate and a crash course in missionary work with Peter are thus ruled out'.

It must have been during this visit that Paul had the spiritual experience described in *Acts* XXII. 17, when, addressing the people from the steps of the Antonia he says: 'And it came to pass, that, when I was come again' (after his conversion) 'to Jerusalem, even while I prayed in the Temple, I was in a trance; and saw him saying unto me, Make haste, and get thee quickly out of Jerusalem: for they will not receive thy testimony concerning me'. That is why the visit was cut short. His friends took him down to Caesarea, the capital, and the splendid port, rivalling Alexandria, which Herod had constructed there. Hence he took ship and went home to Tarsus by way of Syria.

Tarsus was more affluent and flourishing than ever, irradiated by what Pliny calls 'the infinite majesty of the Roman peace'. It was as Strabo describes it, the home of philosophers, with an enthusiasm for education which surpassed that of the Athenians and Alexandrians. The sailmakers, unruly as Dio Chrysostom stigmatizes them, were still numerous, although not full citizens of this proud 'free' self-governing, tribute-exempt

Left:
Peter and Paul, a detail from the great altarpiece by Mantegna in the church of San Zeno Maggiore in Verona. Peter must have looked forward to the encounter with mixed feelings, since hardly three years had passed since Paul's conversion; before that he had been notorious for his persecution of the first Christians.

Facing page:
The site of the Antonia fortress in Jerusalem. While addressing the people from the steps of the Antonia Paul recalls how after his conversion he revisited Jerusalem and 'saw him' (the Lord) 'saying unto me, Make Haste, and get thee quickly out of Jerusalem'. Paul declared that he was in a trance in the Temple when he received the warning (*Acts* XXII. 17–18).

emporium. But to Paul, none of this now meant very much: he had his own work to do. One wonders how his family viewed his new self-given (as it seemed to them) status. They can hardly have welcomed his becoming an itinerant preacher of an alien faith, when all was going so well for them. But Paul's work in the province was unceasing, and it seems to have been fruitful.

To this period must belong at least some of the hard treatment of which he speaks: three shipwrecks, five beatings (thirty-nine strokes at a time) by the Jews, three other floggings, a stoning (which came later), and many another peril. Yet he persevered. And he had his reward. Towards the end of this fourteen-year period, he tells the *Corinthians* (2. XII. 2–9), that fourteen years before the date of

his letter, that is about the year 43, he had been caught up into paradise and had heard unspeakable words, which no man may lawfully utter. Lest he glory, he was afflicted with 'a thorn in the flesh', the mysterious and humiliating disease which he does not specify, 'a messenger of Satan to buffet me'. He three times asked God to release him from it. But the answer came to him: 'My grace is sufficient for thee: for my strength is made perfect in weakness'.

It was: and Paul was soon to prove it, and go on proving it to the end of his days.

CHAPTER THREE

THE FIRST JOURNEY

In the year 41, on 24 January, Caligula was assassinated. The following day, his uncle Claudius was proclaimed emperor. He owed his elevation largely to his old friend Herod Agrippa, grandson of Herod the Great and named after Augustus' minister Marcus Vipsanius Agrippa. Caligula had proclaimed himself divine, and had ordered his statue to be erected in the Temple at Jerusalem. Agrippa, who was in Rome at the time, had at the risk of his life persuaded the half-mad emperor to rescind the order, thereby winning great credit in Jewish eyes. Claudius, out of gratitude, now reconstituted for him the old domain of Herod the Great. The re-establishment of the kingdom brought the Jews of Palestine to the zenith of their earthly felicity. Gone was the procurator, gone were the legions, the eagles, the tax-gatherers. Agrippa behaved perfectly: if in Rome he did as the Romans did, in Jerusalem he was a devout Jew.

As we have seen the original apostles had stayed on in Jerusalem. They were beginning to attract followers, and were likely, as Abel points out, to rival the success of the Hellenists and so to become catalysts of national solidarity; but it was the success of the new faith in Antioch that brought matters to a head. There, the labours of Cypriot and Cyrenian missionaries had brought a number of Greeks into the fold. The chief of these missionaries was Barnabas, a Hellenistic Jew from Cyprus who owned property in Jerusalem. When Antioch, the third city of the empire, became a centre for the adherents of the new Way, it meant that they and their brethren could no longer be regarded as merely another Jewish sect. The citizens of Antioch recognized this: they called them *Christians* (the name occurs here for the first time) Men of Christ; a third race, alongside Greeks and Jews.

This was disturbing news for Herod Agrippa and the orthodox prelates of his capital. The whole movement was subversive, they argued, and might well lead to the overthrow of both secular and ecclesiastical authority. Clearly the leaders must be punished. Agrippa started by executing James, the son of Zebedee, one of those excitable Galileans who so often gave trouble. As a sovereign, if client, king he had authority to do so. This gave great satisfaction to the godly. 'And because he saw it pleased the Jews, he proceeded further to take Peter also.' He intended to have him publicly executed after passover, when Jerusalem would be packed with pilgrims.

One of the seismic shocks to which Jerusalem is prone appears to have wrecked the prison and Peter escaped and fled the city, leaving behind him a few little centres of the new faith, such as the house of Mary, mother of John Mark and aunt of Barnabas, where James the brother of Jesus and the elders used to meet for prayer and fellowship.

On top of this persecution, there followed a disastrous famine, which had been foretold by Agabus, one of the Christian prophets who had come down to Antioch from Jerusalem.

Barnabas, hearing of Paul's missionary labours in Cilicia, had persuaded him to join the nascent

Facing page, above:
There is almost nothing now to be seen of Antioch, the great city on the Orontes which in the empire was next in importance to the mother city and Alexandria. It was in Antioch that the followers of the new Way were first called Christians. The activities of Barnabas were originally concentrated in Antioch, and there the first Gentiles entered the Church. The picture shows part of the modern town.

Below:
Roman remains in Salamis, the site of which lies near modern Famagusta. Barnabas, Paul and John landed at Salamis on the first stage of the first missionary journey.

Right:
A change of autocrat in Rome could have far-reaching effects on the lives of the subjects of the empire. Caligula *(left)* succeeded Tiberius—and was mad enough to want his own image placed in the Temple in Jerusalem. He was dissuaded from this course (which would have provoked rebellion), by the wit of Herod Agrippa who became King Agrippa I of the Jews. Caligula was assassinated after four years misrule, to be succeeded by his despised uncle, Claudius—another circumstance which owed much to Herod Agrippa's quick wits. Claudius *(right)* was to prove a far better ruler than either his predecessor, or his eventual successor, Nero.

Facing page:
James the son of Zebedee and brother of John, called St James the Great, was the first martyr among the apostles. Mantegna's painting shows him before Herod Agrippa (King Agrippa I), by whose order James was beheaded in AD 44.

Barnabas, as portrayed by Botticelli. He was a Jew of Cyprus and one of the first Christians. It was Barnabas who introduced the newly-converted Paul to the Apostles in Jerusalem, and who accompanied Paul on his first journey. There is a tradition that he was martyred at Salamis in Cyprus in AD 61.

church in Antioch, and so Paul had repaired to that splendid city on the river Orontes. Almost nothing of it remains now beyond the great girdle of walls climbing up to the top of Mount Silpius, and a magnificent collection of mosaics rescued by American archaeologists. The rest has gone; the paved streets, the colonnades, the great gateways, overthrown by earthquakes—there were two in Roman times, and a third in 526 which killed a quarter of a million people—and by Sassanian invaders from Persia. Paul had already been in Antioch about a year, working with Barnabas, when Agabus uttered his warning. At once the Christian community there, now the largest and most firmly established in existence, determined to show its loyalty to the mother-church in Jerusalem by sending relief to it, to prove to its members in their spiritual and material distress that their more prosperous brethren remembered them with filial love and gratitude.

To Barnabas and Saul was entrusted this mission of mercy. The exact chronology is as difficult as ever to determine; but it may be that it was while they were in Jerusalem that Agrippa's death occurred. He died in the spring of 44. (Abel would

place the mission two years later: Father Crehan sees 45 as a possible date.) Paul and Barnabas did not tarry long. They went back to Antioch, taking with them John Mark, the cousin of Barnabas who was to be the author of the second Gospel.

One day after their return, while the faithful were gathered for prayer, fasting, the Holy Spirit, speaking no doubt by the mouth of one of the prophets and teachers who were in the assembly (*Acts* XIII. 1) said 'Separate me Barnabas and Saul, for the work whereunto I have called them'. This was to be none other than what is usually known as Paul's First Missionary Journey. Strictly speaking his ministry in Cilicia had been that; but where so much confusion obscures times and seasons, it will be better to stick to the traditional numbering. The generally accepted date is AD 45.

What should the itinerary be? Cyprus had obvious advantages. It was the native country not only of Barnabas but of some of those who had helped to establish the faith in Antioch. Paul may well have had links with Cyprus, quite likely commercial ones, Cilicia being only fifty miles from the island, from which it is easily visible. The harbour town of Antioch was Seleucia-Pieria

at the mouth of the Orontes, where the ruins of the Roman city are still to be seen running out to sea on the lower slopes of the mountain called Musa Dag, and below the town is the little port called al-Mina. It is now, like the ports of Tarsus, Salamis, Perga, Ephesus, Troy and so many others silted up. The reason is a sad one. Deforestation of the heights over the centuries by goats and wood-cutters has caused erosion, which in its turn has caused the precious top-soil to be washed down to the coast, thus ruining both the ports and their hinterland. Conservation was unknown in anti-quity until the days of the emperor Hadrian, who saved the Cedars of Lebanon for posterity.

From Seleucia the two missionaries and their assistant, John, set sail for Salamis near modern Famagusta. It stood on the golden strand that still delights us. Most of what is now visible is late Roman or Byzantine, but the great gymnasium and the baths, like so many Roman baths, almost on the beach itself, help us to realize what grandeur it must have presented to the seaborne visitor.

It was as usual in the synagogues that Paul and Barnabas preached (*Acts* XIII. 5), and they then went through the whole island, bound for Paphos.

Their route would take them by Kitium, the birth-place of Zeno the founder of Stoicism. They would also tarry in many other centres of habitation (Pliny says there were fifteen), preaching their good news in them.

At length they came to Paphos, the seat of the Roman governor. The town had a high reputation among the Romans, because it was the centre of the cult of Venus, or Aphrodite, who had risen from the foam of the sea nearby. Venus was the foundress of the Julian line and her oracle was at Paphos. So famous was it that after a violent earth-quake Augustus had it rebuilt on a new site, and it was to this New Paphos, officially styled Sebaste, that is Augusta, like the Sebaste of Herod the Great in Palestine (Samaria), known as the 'holy metropolis, that Paul and Barnabas came. The Jewish community was wiped out in the time of Trajan, but when Paul and Barnabas visited the island it was considerable, its numbers having been augmented ever since Herod the Great was given the oversight of the copper mines by Augustus.

Here at Paphos occurred a remarkable event. The governor Sergius Paulus (he was a Proconsul) was an intelligent man, and hearing of the activities of the two missionaries sent for them and asked them to expound their doctrine to him. It hap-pened that attached to his court there was a magician (this was quite normal, for all Romans were pathologically superstitious), a Jew called Bar-Jesus. Seeing what an impression Barnabas and Paul were having on his master, he did all in his power to dissuade him from listening to them. Paul, as he is from now on regularly called, rounded on Bar-Jesus, and won the day: Sergius Paulus was converted. The fact that Paul is here so-called in *Acts* for the first time implies that he had invoked his Roman citizenship, the coincidence that he had the same name as the proconsul being an added advantage. There was as yet no official Roman prejudice against a governor becoming a Christian: it was the same as being an adherent of, say, Isis or Pythagoras in the eyes of the ruler.

The two missionaries now crossed the narrow sea between Cyprus and Hither Asia, and made for Perge not, apparently, docking at what was and still is its main port, Attalia, named after king Attalus II of Pergamum (159–138 BC), whose stoa in Athens shews his cultural debt to Greece, but sailing up the river Kestros to Perge. (Attalia became *Adalia* in Turkish, and when in 1928 Turkey abandoned the Arabic script for the Latin, the Greek clerk who did the transliteration, for whom the sound 'd' is represented by 'nt', turned it into *Antalya*, as it now is.)

Perge is for the modern student one of the most interesting cities of all those visited by Saint Paul, and that for two reasons. The first is personal to him, the second to us. In Cyprus, it was Barnabas who was the leader: after all he was in his native country, and he was the conductor of the mission. But at Paphos a subtle change had come over the relationship. There, Paul the Roman citizen had shewn that he must, in that capacity, take precedence in a Roman province. Pamphylia, in which Perge was situated, had been made into a province in AD 42. John Mark, being a sensitive lad, noticed this change of status: his uncle Barnabas now took second place. John resented it: besides he was homesick. He did not see why he should make a certainly tiresome and possibly perilous journey and as a subordinate at that into the uplands, for that is where Paul now decided to go. Very probably, Paul was suffering from a bout of malaria, contracted originally in the Tarsus marshes, and brought on again by the enervating climate of the coastal plain. Paul was unreasonably offended by Mark's decision to go home, as we shall see later on.

A detail of one of the cartoons for Raphael's tapestries woven for the Sistine Chapel. Sergius Paulus sees the blinding of Elymas the sorcerer (*Acts* XIII. 6–12). The duel between the sorcerer and Paul occurred at Paphos and it was there that Paul is so called for the first time. He may in fact have used the Latin form of his name (Saul) because he was dealing with a Roman governor. Sergius Paulus, 'a prudent man', was converted to the new faith.

Below:
This ivory carving comes from a fifth-century casket now in the British Museum. On the left the scene is Iconium, where Thekla listens to Paul discoursing in the house of Onesiphorus. On the right the scene is Lystra, where Paul is stoned by the capricious mob who a little earlier were ready to hail him as a god.

What is so personal to us about Perge is that here, as in Athens and Jerusalem, we can to a large extent actually see the city as Paul saw it. Perge is a typical Hellenistic, Asian city. That is, the old city stood on a hill, or acropolis, just as primitive Athens and Rome did, in accordance with Malthus' first law of population, which enjoins that in troublous times men seek refuge on hills, descending to the plain when security is established. There are scores of examples of such sites in the Levant, but none more eloquent than Perge. The pride of this upper city, which is certainly as old as the seventh century BC, was its sanctuary of Artemis, princess of the city, the goddess who in Callimachus' poem confides that she loves Perge above all other cities including, apparently, Ephesus. Down below is the spacious, tranquil Hellenistic town. As we enter it, we pass between a great theatre, scooped, as such buildings were whenever possible, out of the mountainside and a great stadium, raised on stone vaults. These are in their present form Roman, but no doubt adapted from Greek originals. On the western side of the walled city, which we now enter, there still stands the magnificent Hellenistic town wall, so lofty, with its towers so well preserved, that to an unpractised eye it might well seem medieval. But it is this very wall that greeted the eyes of Paul himself. It gives us a personal connection with him as few other sites do.

To get to his goal, Antioch in Pisidia, Paul had to climb to a plateau more than 3,000 feet above sea level. How did he get there? Professor Lloyd, who knows the whole region intimately, thinks that in Roman times the track due north from Perge was impracticable, and that in any case it would have taken the travellers too far west. Lloyd believes they travelled eastward, along the great trunk road which joined Ephesus and Tarsus, as far as Side, a great commercial port, and thence northward by '. . . the ancient highway across Taurus, which runs by Akşeki and east of the Beyşehir lake. This is a very beautiful road; popular with the Seljuk Turks, who built elaborate stone caravanserais at intervals of one day's journey all along it'.

They reached Antioch in Pisidia, which lies between Yalvac and Akşehir, the latter now a main line station. This lesser Antioch was in no way comparable with a great city such as Perge. Perched up there on the plateau, it was an isolated little town even then, and the arrival of two strangers caused a very considerable stir. Naturally, as was their custom, they attended synagogue on the sabbath, and after the prescribed readings from the Pentateuch and the Prophets, the overseers of the synagogue invited them to give an exhortation. Paul rose, and 'beckoning with his hand' (it was a characteristic gesture of his) addressed himself both to the Jews, and to the 'godfearing', that is those who leaned towards the moral teachings of Judaism, without actually joining Jewry. Paul delivered an eloquent resumé of Jewish history, and ended by declaring that Jesus of Nazareth was the true Messiah, that he was risen from the dead, and that through him all might seek forgiveness of sins. This discourse made a deep impression. Jews, the 'godfearing', even pagans all wanted to hear more. Next sabbath the synagogue was packed. Paul again gave the address, and again delighted and comforted many of his hearers. But his success naturally aroused jealousy, as success always does, and members of the orthodox party denounced Paul and Barnabas (they appear in that order now) as impostors, whereupon Paul made his historic declaration: 'It was necessary that the word of God should first have been spoken to you: but seeing ye put it from you, and judge yourselves unworthy of everlasting life, lo, we turn to the Gentiles'. (Acts XIII. 46.) Yes, it was in this bleak, unregarded little town that this great battle-cry was first uttered. As a result, the gospel was preached throughout all the pagan countryside. But the women of Pisidian Antioch, egged on by the Jews, worked on the feelings of the town notables who turned the newcomers out of the town.

So Paul and Barnabas, 'shook off the dust of their feet against them' and came down to Iconium, modern Konya, following presumably the line of the modern railway. Iconium was then, as it was to become in the days of Islam, and still is, an important centre of commerce much frequented by Jew and Gentile alike. The two missionaries fared here very much as they had done at Antioch. It had by now become the accepted syndrome: welcome, interest, dissension, expulsion. But Paul's stay at Iconium has a special interest, because it was in Iconium that occurred the interlude, as it were, which has given us a not quite contemporary but surely authentic account of Paul's personal appearance. It is contained in a second-century rescension of an earlier document, known as *The Deeds of Paul and Thekla*.

The story concerns the meeting between Paul and a noble lady of Iconium called Thekla. Paul's fame had preceded him, and so it came about that a citizen of Iconium called Onesiphorus, hearing that Paul was about to arrive, went out to meet him and invite him to his house. Never having seen him, he was told to look out for '. . . a man of small

The scene at Lystra when the people were convinced that Paul and Barnabas, having healed a cripple, were gods come down to earth. To the horror of Paul and Barnabas the priests of Zeus (Jupiter in the Authorised Version) prepared a sacrifice to offer them. From a cartoon by Raphael for the tapestry in the Sistine Chapel.

stature, baldheaded, bow-legged, holding himself well, with his eyebrows meeting, and a rather big nose, and full of grace; for at times he looked like a man, and sometimes he had the face of an angel'. In Professor Lloyd's words, 'An affectionate description rather than a flattering one'. The two men met, and that evening Paul preached in Onesiphorus' house.

Now Thekla's parents lived on the other side of the street—one of the narrow alley-ways which still abound in Konya. For several evenings

When Paul was expelled from the city, she followed him from place to place, dressed as a boy, and listened to his teaching. Her disguise being penetrated, she was again arraigned and condemned to all sorts of tortures, from which she was eventually rescued by a certain Tryphaena, a connection of the great Roman Antonine family, one of whose sons was king of Pontus in AD 37. The Antonines owned property in Pisidia. With Tryphaena's help, Thekla found a quiet retreat at Seleucia-in-Cilicia (Selifke) and there devoted herself to Christian teaching. At Mariamlik, near Selifke, a small church was built over the cave in which Thekla lived. In 1955, when Professor Lloyd visited it, only a single fragment of the apse remained, but beneath it the cave was still there. Thekla became the patron saint of Christian teachers. There are many churches dedicated to her in the Orient, and the great western doctors, Ambrose and Augustine, were familiar with her edifying and charming story.

From Iconium Paul and Barnabas made their way to Lystra, some twenty-five miles to the south, a little township of even less importance than Pisidian Antioch. A century earlier, when Cicero had governed Cilicia, it was the haven of brigands.

It happened that at Lystra there was a man who had been a cripple from birth: he was unable to walk. This man was greatly moved by Paul's preaching, so much so that Paul, realizing that the man had faith in him, said to him in a loud voice: 'Stand upright on thy feet'. At once the man leaped up and walked. Thus is the story given in *Acts* XIV, as we now have it. Faith-healing is not unknown in later epochs, though its actual scope is hotly disputed. That Paul must have effected some kind of therapy seems clear from the following verses which relate that the inhabitants, using their own vernacular (Greek would be hardly known in Lystra), cried out that the gods had taken human shape, and they called Barnabas Jupiter, and Paul Mercury, messenger of the gods, because it was he who did all the talking. The priest of Jupiter even went so far as to prepare a sacrifice, with garlands, at the city gate, the immemorial location for a large public assembly.

Paul and Barnabas were scandalized, and did all they could to restrain the people who, familiar as they were with the legend of Philemon and Baucis saw in the epiphany, as it seemed to them, of Paul and Barnabas a realization of the legend. Now came Jews from Iconium, who contrived one of those volte-faces to which popular assemblies are liable (Paul was to witness another, far happier one, in Malta). In no time, they had rounded on

running Thekla sat at a window listening to the voice across the way. Hearing the unseen speaker discourse on virginity (it was one of his favourite themes) Thekla, to the great annoyance of her family, renounced the betrothal they had arranged for her. Her angry parents brought a case against Paul for estrangement. Paul was imprisoned but Thekla, by bribing the warders with a silver mirror, managed to enter his cell and sit at his feet. For this defiance she was condemned to be burned, but was saved by a miraculous storm of rain.

Paul and stoned him, leaving him for dead outside the city. But Paul recovered, and they were able to leave Lystra for Derbe, thirty miles to the south-east. Here they must have stayed for some time, because they made many converts.

From Derbe, it would have been easy for the two companions to return to Tarsus by way of the Cilician Gates, the historic pass through the Taurus mountains, a distance of 150 miles, and so on to Syrian Antioch whence they had set out. But they decided, bravely, that they must revisit and 'confirm' the little churches they had founded on their outward journey. This they did, calling at Lystra, Iconium, Pisidian Antioch and Perge, this last destined to be the Metropolitan see of Pamphylia in due course, a sure sign of Paul's effective foundation. They then took ship at Attalia, and so returned to Syrian Antioch, whence they had set out some five years earlier.

Above, right:
The harbour at Antalya, the Attalia of the New Testament.

Right:
The Turkish village now on the site of Derbe. The little town to the north of the Cilician Gates was Paul and Barnabas' first resting place when Paul recovered from the mob's attack at Lystra.

Far right:
The Cilician Gates, the pass through the Taurus mountains used by travellers from time immemorial and now carrying a modern road. Paul and Barnabas made their way 150 miles by this route from Derbe (modern Degile) to Tarsus.

CHAPTER FOUR

CRISIS AND COMPROMISE
THE SECOND JOURNEY

It was that word *Christian* which caused the trouble. Paul and Barnabas were back in Antioch, and had been there some time, telling in detail all that they had achieved in Asia, and how God had 'opened the door of faith' to the Gentiles. When this came to the ears of the Jerusalem faithful they were greatly perturbed. They were loyal Christians, but at the same time they were loyal Jews. To them it was unthinkable that any man could be a Christian, a follower of Jesus, without first being integrated into Jewry. What *blasphemy*, to abrogate the Law of Moses, the guide and guardian of the Elect for a thousand years. . . . Yet this was clearly what was happening in Antioch, and promulgated as doctrine by the powerful and successful missionaries who operated from that city. Better go and see what these innovators were up to.

It is quite clear both from Luke's account in *Acts* xv. 1–3, and from Paul's own account in *Galatians* II, that this was in no sense an official enquiry, authorised by the reverend leaders in Jerusalem, of whom Peter and James the brother of Jesus were the chief. Luke says merely that 'certain men' came from Jerusalem; Paul, using stronger language (he is writing to the Galatians five years later, expressly to remonstrate with them against being led astray by Judaizers) calls them 'false brethren unawares brought in, who came in privily to spy out our liberty which we have in Christ Jesus, that they might bring us into bondage'.

From this description it looks as though it was some of the die-hards in Antioch itself who had given the first impulse to the enquiry. Paul and Barnabas naturally withstood them. In the end after much debate both parties came to a very sensible decision: they would submit the dispute to the arbitration of the venerable apostles in Jerusalem. Paul went there by an ostentatiously

Gentile route; Tyre, Sidon and Samaria. Did the two parties realize that in coming to this decision they were about to change the whole history of the world? It seems unlikely, but that is in fact what they were doing.

Unfortunately, we have no details of what took place. St Luke, in accordance with current literary practice, gives both Peter and James set-piece speeches, but does not record what Paul, who must have dominated the conference, or Barnabas, actually said. In *Galatians* Paul makes it clear that he did not yield to the Judaizers, some at least of whom were Pharisees of the stricter observance. Peter has already admitted a pagan centurion to the fold, as related in *Acts* x. He is therefore presented as being conciliatory to Paul. So is James: Gentile converts should merely be required to abstain from eating meat offered to idols (for what would be a participation in heathen sacrifices), from foods which had blood in them, or had been prepared from strangled carcases, and from fornication. According to *Acts* xv. 25–7 these sensible, compromise, resolutions were embodied in a letter, to be carried to Antioch 'by our beloved Barnabas and Paul', with other members of the Jerusalem congregation to explain things by word of mouth. They did not wish the brethren at Antioch to get the impression that Paul had forced through his own solution, in the face of what was after all a genuine difference of opinion.

The question was not there and then settled once and for all. Paul tells us the assembly dissolved

'If thou, being a Jew, livest after the manner of Gentiles, and not as do the Jews, why compellest thou the Gentiles to live as do the Jews?' Paul reproaches Peter for his inconsistency, the incident described in *Galatians* II. II. From the painting by Guido Reni, now in the Brera Gallery in Milan.

in complete amity, he and Barnabas being given the 'right hand of fellowship', with an injunction not to forget the poor with which Paul was again most eager to comply. But the supremely important point which Paul had gained was that while the Jerusalem elders would be primarily concerned to win their fellow Jews, Paul and Barnabas were free—more, had an express mandate—to turn to the Gentiles. True, a little later, when Peter came to Antioch, Paul upbraided him, because after at first sharing a common table with Gentiles, when some of James' associates came to Antioch, he stopped doing so for fear of giving offence. Barnabas did the same. Paul charged Peter with inconsistency. If Peter, a Jew, had been willing to live as a Gentile, why did he now try to force Gentiles to live as Jews?

This difference between two apostles continued to puzzle the godly for many years to come. As late as the fourth century it led to a sharp divergence of opinion between St Jerome, who regarded the whole episode as fabricated by Peter and Paul in order to make Paul's stand plain to all men, and his contemporary Augustine who easily demolished so specious an hypothesis. Luke, writing fifteen years after the event, when the once burning question was as cold as clinker, simply omits the episode altogether. It was no longer relevant.

The enormous importance of the conference is admirably summed up by Bornkamm (Ch. 4, *ad fin*):

'The outcome of the apostolic assembly is important for theology, for the history of the church, and for world history alike. It shows that the church's unity had not fallen in pieces. The danger that the mother church would harden into a sect of Judaism and that Hellenistic Christianity would dissolve into a welter of non-historical mystery cults had been averted.'

That both Paul and Luke realized the paramount importance of the Jerusalem conference is clear from the manner in which each has recorded it: it was beyond doubt the most significant event in the history of the primitive church. Paul devotes an unusual amount of space to it when writing to the Galatians, and employs the most downright language in describing his own stand. Luke's account in *Acts* is noteworthy not only because of its literary artistry, but because of its placing. It occupies, as Bornkamm reminds us, a key position right in the middle of the book: it forms as it were a watershed. Until the assembly, everything had turned on the Jerusalem church and its leading figures, Peter in particular. After it, these figures disappear, and the sole subject of the narrative is the work of Paul.

Luke, generally accepted as the author of the third Gospel and the Acts of the Apostles. The portrayal is that by Domenico Ghirlandaio, from a series of frescoes in the Palazzo Vecchio in Florence. The style of his writings suggest that Greek was his native language, and he is 'the beloved physician' of *Colossians* IV. 14 He accompanied Paul from Troas to Philippi on his second journey. The bull (more familiarly a calf) symbol is traditional and based on *Revelation* IV. 6–9.

Facing page, left:
Mark, the author of the second Gospel, was also the young 'John, whose surname was Mark' of *Acts* XV. 37 who turned back during the first journey with Paul and Barnabas and therefore lost the approval of Paul. Mark was Barnabas' nephew and he accompanied his uncle on further journeys. This mosaic is from St Mark's Cathedral in Venice.

Right:
Paul's next companion was Silas, who was probably the 'Silvanus, a faithful brother unto you' to whom Peter gave his first Epistle for transmission from Rome. A mosaic from the Baptistery, St Mark's in Venice.

It is easy to imagine how heart-lifting, indeed inspiring, the outcome of the conference must have been to Paul. It was no doubt at this juncture that he began to conceive of his mission as world-wide —no longer confined to his homeland and the adjacent regions. But naturally these Asian con-

gregations—we may now begin to call them churches—were particularly dear to him, as being his firstborn in Christ. From which it follows that he was eager to revisit them.

At the end of the year 49, or early in 50, he decided to do so. Again he suggested to Barnabas that he should be his companion, to '... visit our brethren in every city where we have preached the word of the Lord, and see how they do'. Barnabas agreed, but wanted to take with him his nephew John Mark. Paul was still resentful of John's desertion during the former journey, and refused to take him along with them. Suppose he forsook them a second time? The two missionaries had so sharp a contention over the matter—what Luke, using a medical term, calls a 'paroxysm'—that they 'departed asunder one from the other'.

So they went their separate ways, Barnabas taking John Mark, and Paul Silas, who was one of the two delegates of the Jerusalem church charged with explaining the conference's decisions to Antioch. Barnabas went back to Cyprus, where his memory is honoured in a great church hard by Salamis. We hear no more of his labours. Happily, we do know that Paul made it up both with him and with John Mark; he later refers to both of them with affection, and expresses the hope that Mark will rejoin him.

This time, Paul and Silas travelled by land, and once again Professor Lloyd is our guide. The two missionaries crossed the Amanus mountains and passing through Cilicia came to Tarsus. Everywhere they went, they 'confirmed the churches'. From Tarsus their route lay northwards through the famous pass known as the Cilician Gates. At its narrowest point, the Romans actually installed a real gate, with a guard stationed to open and shut it. Long before, Xenophon had noted that it had to be 'disencumbered of fallen stones' before an army could pass through it. Far up on a crag above it there stands a medieval castle, still owned by the Gülek family who gave the pass its Turkish name.

Paul had now climbed some 3,000 feet since leaving Tarsus. He and Silas emerged from the Gates onto the plateau, where it would be fairly easy going to reach Derbe, Lystra and Iconium. In each place they told the nascent churches to which Paul was so deeply attached of the decisions of the Jerusalem conference. Many a mind must have been set at rest by the news, many a heart cheered. There could be no doubt any more: they were Christians by right, not proselytes of Judaism, nor poor relations of Jewry.

Paul and Silas now turned north with the idea of preaching in Bithynia, that is the region of Asia Minor immediately to the east of the Bosphorus.

It is chiefly renowned in history as having been the native land of Antinoüs, the tragic favourite of the emperor Hadrian, and of the great Roman historian, who wrote in Greek, Dio Cassius. But something hindered them: they were forbidden to go there by the Holy Spirit, who had already placed Asia 'out of bounds' to them. How one would like to know what really went on in Paul's mind at this juncture. Had he already decided that his goal must be the west, Greece, even Rome itself? This is the most probable explanation. After all, the leaven had been implanted in Galatia: would not the Gospel spread from there, were not his own churches to be missionary? His own duty was surely to put his trust in his children in Christ, and to press on to regions which as yet knew Him not. The two companions now proceeded by way of Dorylaeum, modern Eskişehir. They skirted round the north of Mysia, and came down to the Aegean at Alexandria-Troas, just below old Troy itself, standing on that ghost-haunted peninsula from which across the Dardanelles the pilgrim describes the gleaming memorials of a later but equally tragic encounter.

It was at Troas that Paul beheld the vision which was to mould not only Paul's destiny but that of Europe as well. 'There stood a man of Macedonia, and prayed him saying, Come over into Macedonia, and help us.' From this point on, we encounter the 'we' passages of *Acts*, which identify the author of the book. Was Luke also the 'man of Macedonia' of the vision? He was certainly there in Troas. The party now consisted of Paul, Silas, Luke and young Timothy, whom Paul had brought with him from Lystra. They sailed north-west, between Imbros and Cape Helles, and so came to Samothrace.

This island had long been renowned; since the Trojan war, at the least, for it was from the summit of Samothrace, 5,000 feet above the sea, that Poseidon watched the struggle. It was a centre of worship, to which postulants flocked, bearing rich offerings, from all over the Hellenic world. They must have been ardent and determined, because Pliny remarks that Samothrace was the 'most harbourless' island of them all. It still is, and visitors are lucky if they are able to land. The aspect of the island is European, green and wooded. It has all the amenities of a Greek *polis*, including a theatre above which stood on her ship's prow of marble the famous Winged Victory now in the Louvre. Paul must indeed have felt that he had entered a new world·in the West, as indeed he had. The party made but a brief call at Samothrace, and 'the next day' moved on to the mainland, landing at Neapolis, now known as Kavalla.

Neapolis was the terminal port of the great Via Egnatia, which linked the Adriatic and the Aegean. It was a vital artery in the Roman body politic. Beyond the Adriatic lay the Via Appia, which led to Rome. Generals, merchants, proconsuls, all used this grand highway. It was fitting therefore that the Gospel, too, should make its entry into Europe by the same gateway.

The present aspect of Neapolis is unique in Greece. The town is built on two hills round the modern harbour. The dip between the two hills

Below:
The remnants of Troy—not the city of the *Iliad* but of the much later Hellenistic and Roman city. Just below Troy, at Troas, Luke and Timothy joined Paul and Silas and the four of them sailed for Samothrace.

Below, right:
The modern Greek port of Kavalla was Neapolis in ancient times, and it was there that Paul first set foot in Europe. One of the great Roman roads, that to the east, the Via Egnatia, terminated at Neapolis. The harbour lies between two hills; the depression between them is spanned by the arches of a Roman aqueduct.

is spanned by the arches of a Roman aqueduct; but on the eastern hill, silhouetted against the blue horizon, stands a great statue of a Muslim monarch and nearby is that monarch's palace. He was Muhammad Ali, the founder of the dynasty which ruled Egypt in the nineteenth and early twentieth centuries. Kavalla was his birthplace, and in the days when there was a large and flourishing Greek colony in Egypt, the Greek government prudently allowed the Egyptian royal house to renovate and adorn the birthplace of their founder. The ancient name of the city still survives in the title of the Diocesan bishop, who is styled Metropolitan of Philippi and Neapolis.

It was for Philippi that the apostolic wayfarers were bound. We to-day can follow them, along the eight miles which separate the port from the capital (of the region, not the whole province of Macedonia: that was Thessalonika). Philippi owes its name to Philip II of Macedon, father of Alexander the Great, whose mother Olympias he had met on Samothrace. Philip was interested in the gold which in early days was washed down by the neighbouring rivers. The old name of the town, indeed, was Krenides (fountains); but Philip fortified it and gave it his own name. When the Romans came, Philippi gained a new importance from its position on the Via Egnatia. To most of us the name is familiar from Shakespeare's *Julius Caesar*, for it was here in the year 42 BC that Augustus, as he was to become, and Antony, whom he was to eliminate eleven years later, defeated Brutus and Cassius, the last of the Republicans. In gratitude Augustus made Philippi a 'colony', that is a little Rome from Rome, with privileged citizenship and freedom from fiscal exactions, like Tarsus. Philippi therefore has the double distinction of having been the seed-bed both of the Roman empire and of the Christian church in Europe. To-day, Philippi bears ample testimony to both. The excavated remains of the ancient city display not only a fine theatre and a magnificent forum, but the foundations of three great basilicas.

The Jewish community in Philippi was small, so small that they had no synagogue. They therefore met for their sabbath services in a little open-air oratory on the bank of a stream, water being necessary for the ritual purification prescribed by the Law (cf. *John* II. 6—the marriage at Cana).

Paul and his companions went there too, and started to talk with the women—we are in the West now, and women are not segregated or veiled, as they would be in the Orient. One of these was a business-woman from Thyátira. Her name was Lydia and she traded in purple cloth, that being the staple commerce of the town. She was a devout soul drawn to monotheism. Paul's preaching convinced her that this message was the true guide.

Luke was still with the others. He records that one day, as they went to prayer, they met a girl who possessed second sight—or what passed for it. She was exploited by her owners, who made a good living by her. Just the sort of case to interest Luke the physician. Apparently the girl was much attracted by Paul and his companions and used to

follow them about, calling on one and all to recognize them as servants of God. Paul, no doubt after consulting Luke, decided that the poor girl was a dupe, and that it was his duty to put an end to the imposture and free her from this psychopathic incubus. He did so by instilling into her a genuine faith, which was able to expel the bogus hallucination so carefully fostered by her proprietors. She stopped telling fortunes, 'soothsaying' as it was ironically called.

Her masters were furious. How were they to get a living now? They caught Paul and Silas, and dragged them into the market-place. 'These men, being Jews,' they said, 'do exceedingly trouble our city, and teach customs, which are not lawful for us to receive, neither to observe, being Romans.' It was cleverly done—the implications were far-reaching, with an immediate appeal to the narrow and the bigoted.

The mob was all out for a bit of Jew-baiting. The local magistrates, (for the city being 'free' had its own little senate) at once ordered Paul and Silas to be arrested. Luke was no longer there, having temporarily left Philippi on personal business of his own. Paul and Silas were duly interrogated— as it would be said nowadays; that is beaten up, and put in the 'security' section of the prison. At midnight, they called a little prayer-meeting and sang some hymns. The other prisoners listened to them. Suddenly there was an earthquake. The doors

sprang open, the stocks in which the prisoners were held fell apart. The poor head warder, fearing a big gaol-break, was about to kill himself. Paul, as so often, took command of the situation. 'Do thyself no harm:' he cried out, 'for we are all here.' The poor man called for a light and dashed in and knelt before Paul and Silas. There must be something in their kind of salvation, after all. Paul explained what it was. The warder was baptized, with his family. He gave his prisoners something to eat, and washed their wounds.

As soon as it was day, he went off to the magistrates. After a little deliberation they sent the beadles to tell the warder to let Paul and Silas go. But Paul said: 'They have beaten us openly uncondemned, being Romans, and have cast us into prison: and now do you thrust us out privily? Nay verily; but let them come themselves and fetch us out'. When the beadles reported this to the magistrates, they were appalled. *Romans?* They brought Paul and Silas out of prison, and begged them to go away. They didn't want to get into trouble with the Romans. Paul and Silas went back to Lydia's house to say goodbye, and then departed on the road to Thessalonika.

Paul always cherished the happiest and proudest memories of this first Christian church in Europe. Writing to them fifteen years later, he uses terms of special endearment. 'For God is my record how greatly I long after you all,' and 'Therefore, my brethren dearly beloved and longed for, my joy and crown, so stand fast in the Lord, my dearly beloved.'

Once again Paul had proved that he could be a Roman, could be a minister of Christ, but also a very human being.

The ruins of Philippi, the city which owed its prominence and its name to Philip of Macedon, who was acutely aware of its use as a centre for collecting alluvial gold from the nearby rivers. In Christian tradition Philippi has a special place – it was here that the first Christian community in Europe was established. Paul's Epistle to the Philippians demonstrates the particular affection he held for them.

Above, left:
Thessalonika, from the time of its foundation in 315 BC, has been a thriving city and seaport and a place where people of many races meet. The illustration shows the remains of the arch of Galerius, the emperor 'of the east' under Diocletian who persecuted the Christians while he held power but was forced to reconsider his policy when he encountered the opposition of Constantine and defeat in Italy. His death saw the beginning of the Christians' complete recognition as the religion of the empire.

CHAPTER FIVE

THE SECOND JOURNEY
HELLAS UNBOUND

On leaving Philippi the three comrades, Paul, Silas and Timothy made for Amphipolis, the 'town between two rivers', so-called because it stood on a little peninsula formed by the river Struma, near its discharge into lake Tachynos. Pliny says it was a free city and later, under the emperor Diocletian, it became the capital of Eastern Macedonia; but it never achieved the importance of its neighbour Philippi. It is still called Amphipoli. Their next staging post was the town of Apollonia, whence passing within a few miles of Aristotle's birthplace, Stagira, they came to Thessalonika, then as now a great centre of commerce and communications, for it too bestrode the Via Egnatia, besides being, as it still is, Greece's gateway to the north, and a thriving seaport.

The city had been founded in 315 BC by one of Alexander the Great's generals, Cassander. He married Alexander's sister and tactfully called his new foundation by her name. It continued to flourish under the Romans and was the seat of the Proconsul of the province. It had its own City Council, or *demos*, of which the executive officers were in Paul's day five or six *politarchs*, as Luke describes them in the original Greek, a striking example of his accuracy. At one time it was thought that Luke had simply coined the word; but inscriptions have now confirmed that the officers were called by the title Luke gives them.

The population of Thessalonika was a mixture of all sorts and conditions of many races (which is why the French word *macédoine* means a fruit salad or a dish of mixed vegetables). There was then, as now, a large Jewish community in the city. A little to the south and inland, rose Berea (now Veroia) a little out-of-the-way town, as Cicero calls it, on the left bank of the river Haliac-mon (Vistritza). A little to the south again rises Mount Olympus, home of the gods. Berea was the first city to open its gates to the victorious Romans after the decisive battle of Pydna (168 BC). A great company of Jews, and the pagan pantheon—Paul had much to contend with in Thessalonika.

As was his custom, Paul started in the synagogue, where on three successive sabbaths he disputed with the Jews, trying to convince them that Jesus really was their promised Messiah. He had small success. He must have been disappointed as well as tired; because as we learn from his letters to the *Thessalonians* (1. II. 9 & 2. III. 8) he laboured 'night and day, because we would not be chargeable unto any of you'—that is, so as not to be a burden to anyone. And that after walking nearly a hundred miles from Philippi. His good friends in that town came to the rescue, and sent him material help on at least two occasions (*Philippians* IV. 16).

There were however compensations: a large number of pagans, and the now usual band of women adhered to the new faith. This infuriated the orthodox Jews who staged a demonstration, manned as such events often are by ruffians, and besieged the house of Jason where the missionaries were lodging. Not finding them, they dragged Jason and others of the brethren before the politarchs, and accused them of sedition (this was the most dangerous accusation possible in a Roman province: it had been paramount in bringing Jesus of Nazareth to the cross), and of saying that 'there is another king, one Jesus'. The politarchs, who were probably fairly familiar with this sort of uproar in

The Roman agora (market place) in Athens with, in the background, the Acropolis. It was *Roman* Athens that Paul knew though it was outwardly the city of Perikles. He preached in the agora.

their huge cosmopolis, merely bound over Jason and his companions.

But the brethren, being sensible, at once sent off Paul and Silas by night to Berea. The people were 'more noble' than those of the big city, and received the newcomers and their message kindly. There were the usual debates in the synagogue, and preaching to pagans outside. Many, both Jews and Gentiles, men and women, accepted the new faith. This again drove the Jews of Thessalonika into action: the little town was not 'out of the way' enough for safety. The Jews came to Berea, and stirred up more trouble. There was nothing for it: Paul must go. The brethren got him down to the not so distant coast, and put him on board a coasting vessel bound for Athens. Silas and Timothy stayed on to look after the new converts, an interesting sidelight on the relative impact made by Paul and his companions.

Paul's ship is traditionally, and reasonably, held not to have docked at either of the harbours of Phaleron, now Pashalimani and Turkolimani, nor in the splendid haven of Piraeus, but to have moored in the bay which lies between present north Athens and the airport. Where he lodged we do not know, but we do know that like most Athenians ancient and modern he passed much of his time in the open air. The Athens he beheld was still outwardly the 'violet-crowned' city of Perikles. Plutarch, writing some half-century after Paul's visit, thus describes Perikles' creations: 'They were created in a short time to last for a long time. Each one of them, in its beauty, was there and then an antique; but even to-day it has the flower and freshness of something newly wrought. There is a perennial bloom of youth about them, as though the unfaltering breath of an ageless spirit had been breathed into them'.

Many of them we can still behold—the temple of Wingless Victory, the Propylaea, the Parthenon, the Erectheion, on one side, and the Theatre of Dionysus on the other and down below the Temple of Hephaistos, miscalled the Theseum. Paul would see also some later embellishments, the stoas of Attalus and Eumenes, kings of Pergamum; the Choragic Monument, the Tower of the winds, and the fine Roman Forum which still survive. He would also have seen many of the buildings in the Agora, including the Painted Stoa, which have disappeared; while we see many, such as Hadrian's great Olympeium, the archway to his new city, and the stadium and concert-theatre of Herodes Atticus which were only built in the second century AD.

All these treasures still invigorate us. They are heart-lifting, they fill us with a joy as keen as it is innocent, a joy all the more poignant because the heart of Athens is now obscured by a concrete and plaster sprawl that has engulfed its twin rivers the famous Ilissus and the Eridanus—they are both sewers now—and much of the surrounding countryside from Sunium to Eleusis.

Paul's emotion was the opposite of ours. To Paul these buildings were not beautiful monu-

The Stoa of Attalus II of Pergamum (159–138 BC), restored by the American School of Athens, has the exact dimensions and details—even marble from the original quarries—which Paul would have known. The work of restoration was begun in 1953 and completed in 1956.

ments raised by man's spiritual genius but the embodiment of wickedness, the shrines of false gods, whence proceeded all that was in his eyes evil. Equally evil, if not more so, were the innumerable statues and altars which lined the Sacred Way, linking the Double Gate and the cemetery just outside it in the Potters' Quarter (*Kerameikos*, whence our 'ceramics') with the Acropolis. It was up this steep road that the Panathenaic procession climbed every four years to pay honour and worship to the Maiden-goddess Athena, protectress of the city, whose statue of gold and ivory, the masterpiece of Pheidias, welcomed her votaries—citizens, denizens, magistrates, priests, musicians, virgins bearing offerings, animals for sacrifice, and young men on horseback escorting

the cortège. It is this procession that the famous frieze, the controversial Elgin marbles, represents.

It must strike us with bewilderment that anyone could regard such 'Attic shapes' as other than the acme of pure, unsullying beauty. But it is essential to our understanding of Paul's mission in Athens, and its comparative failure, to grasp the basic fact that for Paul all this display was a blasphemous violation of the Law of God.

The narrative in *Acts* XVII suggests that Paul was unwell after leaving Berea; the friends who had taken him to the coast had accompanied him all the way to Athens. He felt lonely: he begged them to send Silas and Timothy to him as quickly as possible. Meanwhile he did as he usually did, he attended the synagogue and delivered his message

in it. But being in Athens, he also did as the Athenians did. This outward conformity was one of his principles, provided it did not conflict with any of his others. So we find Paul in the Agora.

Athens was an untidy city. Not a bit like Piraeus, which had been entirely remodelled by Perikles on a plan drawn up by the most famous town-planner of the day, Hippodamus of Miletus. This genius from the city of geniuses, was an adept at designing towns on the grid-plan. Alexander the Great passed through one town in Asia Minor laid out on the Hippodamian plan, Priene, not far from Miletus itself. He liked the design so much, that he adopted it for his own Alexandria. After being dormant for many centuries, the chessboard design was revived in the sixteenth century at Puebla de los Angeles in Mexico, whence it came back to Europe to give us its most beautiful modern embodiment, Valetta in Malta. It also in due course gave us New York. But Athens it never did give us—the city was too cluttered up with shrines and holy enclosures by the time of Perikles.

So people tended to spend their time in the Agora, which was itself a holy enclosure, with boundary-stones, some of which are still there. As to what went on there, besides housing the secular offices of the state, it was the commercial centre of Athens. As the old comic poet Euboulus said: 'You'll find everything sold together in the same place at Athens: figs, witnesses to summonses, bunches of grapes, turnips, pears, apples, givers of evidence, roses, medlars, porridge, honeycombs, chick peas, law-suits, beestings, myrtle, allotment-machines [for filling juries], irises, lambs, water-clocks, laws, indictments'.

During the first century BC Athens, in common with other Greek cities, had suffered great tribulation from which it had only partially recovered. In 86 BC it had been captured and sacked, with appalling loss of life, by the Roman general Sulla. Forty-one years later, a friend of Cicero's wrote to him: 'On my return from Asia, I was sailing from Aegina towards Megara. Behind me was Aegina, in front Megara, Piraeus to the right, Corinth to the left, all at one time flourishing towns, now lying prostrate and in ruins before my eyes'.

True, the city had to some extent recovered its

Raphael's cartoon for his tapestry *St Paul preaching to the Athenians* could hardly be said to capture a feeling for first-century Athens; but it is one of the few representations by a great painter. The Athenians listened to Paul with mild interest, and found him wanting; Greek religious thought gave no place to a punisher and they could make nothing of judgment and repentance.

outward aspect, and both Julius Caesar and the emperor Augustus had contributed to the cost of building the Roman forum, in return for which the Athenians had erected a circular temple to Augustus and Rome on the Acropolis itself. His great minister, Marcus Vipsanius Agrippa, had given them a concert-hall, and had been rewarded with a statue before the Propylaea, the plinth of which still stands. But the old spirit was gone. Indeed, the island of Rhodes was now the cultural centre of Hellas. Cicero, Cassius, Horace, the emperor Tiberius himself, had all studied philosophy and oratory in Rhodes. The so-called philosophy of Athens was little more than clever chat. St Luke says that both the citizens and their visitors spent their whole time in gossip.

When therefore we hear that 'certain philosophers of the Epicureans and Stoics' met Paul, we are prepared for their supercilious attitude towards him. 'What will this babbler say?' (*Acts* XVII. 18). Both these schools of thought had long been established in Athens. They had become its most famous; though as we have seen Greek philosophy sprang not from Athens but from Ionia, and neither Epicurus nor Zeno, founder of Stoicism, was an Athenian by birth.

Epicurus was born in 341 BC in Samos, just off the coast of Ionia, of Athenian parents. When he was twenty-one, the Athenian settlers were expelled from Samos by one of Alexander's generals. After being a refugee for fifteen years, Epicurus came to Athens, established himself and his school in a garden on the outskirts of the city, and lived there in happy seclusion until his death in 270 BC. His pupils, who included slaves and women, were devoted to him. His philosophy was based on the atomic theory of Democritus, which held that evolution was a purely natural process with which gods have nothing to do. Gods there may be, but they are utterly unconcerned with man; it follows therefore that any concept of punishment is folly. There is no heaven either beyond the grave.

Epicurus' teaching was a philosophy of escape, of quietism—*ataraxía*, peace and quiet, that was to be the goal. Noble natures might find in this doctrine a guide to the contemplative life but for the vulgar majority it seemed to countenance self-indulgence, which is why our word 'epicure' means what it does. Two great poets of antiquity were Epicureans, Horace, gentlest of them all, and Lucretius, whose atomic epic on *The Nature of Things* is the greatest of its kind in any language. It helped to inspire Virgil, and is reflected in many of our own poets including Gray and Tennyson.

Far different was the origin of Stoicism. Its founder, Zeno, was not a Greek, but a Semite, the son of a Phoenician merchant of Kitium in Cyprus. Ugly, feeble, and dusky-hued, he was nicknamed 'the Egyptian'. He reached Athens in 314 BC, that is nine years before Epicurus, as a shipwrecked pauper. In a bookshop in Athens he came upon Xenophon's *Memoirs of Sokrates*; he decided then and there to study philosophy. For thirteen years he sat at the feet of Krates, the leading philosopher of the day. He became a philosopher himself in 301. Being too poor to hire a hall, he taught in the famous Painted Porch or Stoa, at the northern end of the Agora, just beyond the existing Metropolitana railway, where Polygnotus had depicted the defeat of the Persians. Hence his disciples were called Stoics.

As already noted Zeno was a Semite, and the mark of all Semitic doctrine from Isaiah to Muhammad is an uncompromising belief in eternal order, combined with an intolerance of the imperfect amounting to a sense of sin. In the eyes of a Stoic there is nothing fortuitous about the universe: it is governed by an immutable law which it is wicked to transgress. The law of the universe must be also the law of our own natures, and we can only realize ourselves by conforming to the divine purpose, whose service is perfect freedom. Among the greatest exponents of Stoicism in the first century was Seneca, one of that group of Spanish-born Romans who had so profound an influence on Roman life and letters in the first two centuries of our era. He wrote: 'Each of us has two fatherlands, one the country in which we happen to be born, the other an empire upon which the sun never sets'. The Epicureans denied Providence: for the Stoics it was the ruler of the world.

That Paul was acquainted with Stoicism, we have already seen. He was familiar with its terminology, if not with its doctrine. He could quote a Stoic hymn, as we shall shortly see. The Stoic echoes in Paul's letters early led men to believe that he had actually corresponded with Seneca. When therefore Paul met the representatives of the two rival philosophies, it is easy to guess that he would find himself more in sympathy with the Stoics than with the Epicureans; but the real trouble was that basically he had no true sympathy with either. To Paul, the paintings in the Porch were just as much an abomination, a breach of the second commandment, as were the city's 20,000 statues (Pliny's estimate) in the round.

When therefore representatives of either persuasion, Epicurean and Stoic, asked him to explain his novel ideas, Paul was in a quandary. They led him up to the Hill of Ares (the Greek god often

Zeno, the philosopher who taught in the Stoa and gave the Stoic ideas to the world. A Semite, Zeno was born at Kitium in Cyprus, and it is interesting that two of his most distinguished successors came from Tarsus–the city of Paul. Zeno's basic teaching was that the only real good is virtue, the only real evil moral weakness. The Stoics of Athens paid more attention to Paul than most of his listeners: 'We will hear thee again of this matter' (*Acts* XVII, 32).

identified with Mars), just below the Acropolis. It had formerly been the abode of the Furies, and later became the venue for sittings of the supreme court of Athens, the Areopagus. (To-day, the name appears in Greek on a brass plate affixed to what was formerly the Athenian home of Schliemann, the discoverer of Troy, which now houses the supreme court—a typical example of the Greek sense of continuity.) The court no longer sat there on the Hill—it had been used as a police-post—which has led some scholars to believe that Paul was summoned to appear in the royal portico down by the temple of Hephaistos, where the court then assembled. But there is no hint of this in *Acts*. Luke, accurate as usual, says that the philosophers took him and brought him 'unto' the Hill of Ares. That is, they wanted a quiet spot for a little discussion, away from the hurly-burly of the Agora. On the hill, cut into the rock, there were two seats, one for the prosecutor and the other for the defending counsel, with a semicircular tribune for the judges in between. So now the two groups arranged themselves on the judges' bench, and 'Paul stood in the midst of Mars' hill' (*Acts* XVII. 22).

After congratulating them on being 'thoroughly godfearing' (the A.V. rendering 'too superstitious' is a mistranslation, as is also that of the inscription Paul describes in the following Verse), Paul takes as his theme an altar he had seen inscribed 'to an unknown god'. That was the God he had come to declare to them. He was a God who lived not in man-fashioned temples (such as those examples before their eyes), nor did he need offerings (such as those presented on the innumerable Athenian altars). He gave life to one and all, equally; and here Paul quoted the poet Aratus: 'For in him we live and move and have our being; as certain of your own poets have said; (the line appears substantially the same in Cleanthes as well) 'For we are also his offspring'.

That was all quite tolerable to philosophic ears, but it was not what Paul was there to say. He now got to his point. God had overlooked human frailties for some time, but he now called on everybody to repent and be prepared to meet the great judge. This puzzled his hearers. Repentance to meet a great judge? What was this strange man talking about? Greek ideas about sin and repentance were vague, to say the least. The nearest they could get to 'sin' was *amartia*, 'missing the target', for which the best remedy was *metanoia*, a change of mind. All quite logical, but how far from the Judaeo-Christian concepts of sin, penitence, and repentance! Paul was using the current terminology to express ideas which were by no means current. He went farther. The judge was to be a man whom God had ordained, and whom, as a guarantee of his authority, raised from the dead.

That was too much for the philosophers. Some —the Epicureans— were scandalized. Had not Epicurus himself said: 'Therefore Death, the king of terrors, is nothing to us, because as long as we exist Death is not present, and when death is come, we are no more'? They simply mocked Paul —they wouldn't listen to any more. On the other hand there were those, Stoics, no doubt, who caught echoes of their own doctrine in what Paul had said. They told him they'd like to hear him again, presumably in the absence of those who mocked.

The meeting broke up. Paul left for Corinth soon after. His labours in Athens had been disappointing, but not wholly unfruitful. A small group had been converted including a member of the Areopagus itself called Dionysius and a noble lady called Damaris. This was a meagre harvest but Paul, as we shall shortly see, realized that he had gone about things the wrong way, and must change his methods if he was to be the apostle to the Gentiles.

CHAPTER SIX

THE SECOND JOURNEY CORINTH

Paul must have had much to occupy his mind during the short journey from Athens to Corinth. Athens had been a failure—the first real failure he had experienced in a decade and a half of fruitful work. How much this weighed on Paul's spirit is indicated by his failure to refer to it in his letters; the exception occurs almost in parenthesis in his first surviving letter, that to the Thessalonians (1 *Thessalonians* III. 1), written from Corinth. He says nothing of what he did in Athens, merely that he was alone. What a contrast to the almost baroque exuberance of Luke's famous narrative, a contrast so complete that Bornkamm can write 'Only when we come to Corinth do we find ourselves once more on the firm ground of history'. And this is how Paul himself describes his arrival there, in one of several letters he wrote later on from Ephesus to his Corinthian converts (1 *Corinthians* II. 1–4):

'And I, brethren, when I came to you, came not with excellency of speech or of wisdom, declaring unto you the testimony of God. For I determined not to know anything among you, save Jesus Christ, and him crucified. And I was with you in weakness, and in fear, and in much trembling. And my speech and my preaching was not with enticing words of man's wisdom, but in demonstration of the Spirit and power.' A remarkable self-analysis indeed. Riots, beatings, false imprisonment—he could put up with those as occupational risks; but this was something different: the fault had lain with Paul himself. As the above-quoted passage shews, he was determined to correct it. Corinth was an ideal place to do it.

Corinth was in every way the complete opposite of Athens, except in the majesty of its setting. The Greek city lay at the foot of Acrocorinth, which is 1,500 feet high. Far from being crowned by a temple of a virgin-protectress like Athens, it supported a shrine of Aphrodite wherein according to Strabo (VIII. 6.2) more than a thousand dedicated prostitutes followed their calling. Down below lay the city, on two levels. The upper was occupied by a Doric temple of Apollo built in the sixth century BC; the lower by the agora, the stadium and the rest of the town. The walls extended for five miles, or eleven counting those of Acrocorinth.

Corinth enjoyed two advantages which made her unique. The first was her position on the isthmus. All road-traffic from north to south must cross it. Moreover she controlled not one harbour but two, giving her access to both Aegean and Adriatic; and to avoid the hazards of sailing round the Peloponnese merchantmen would unload at one end of the isthmus, carry their cargoes across it and reload at the other end in another ship; or drag the ships overland on sledges running in a marble tramway, of which traces survive at the western end. (The canal, which Nero tried in vain to excavate, was opened in 1893. It is just under four miles long.) The second advantage which Corinth enjoyed, so rare in Greece, was and still is an abundant water-supply. Thus endowed, Corinth very early became a famous emporium and entrepôt. It established colonies in the western Mediterranean, including Syracuse itself. Corinthian pottery was a staple export from early times, the decoration being influenced by themes imported on textiles from the farther east.

Corinth was also famous for its bronzes, and for

The great city of Corinth was completely destroyed by the Roman general Mummius in 146 BC and the remains visible today are those of the Roman city of Julius Caesar. The great rock is Acrocorinth, the original citadel of the city, just as the Acropolis was the citadel of Athens.

the third order of Greek architecture, namely the Corinthian, with its richly foliated capital, said to have been inspired by an acanthus plant which had sprung up on the tomb of a maiden round the circular box of trinkets deposited upon it by her faithful nurse.

But the famous and opulent Greek city was not the one which greeted the eyes of Paul: it had been totally destroyed by the Roman general Mummius in 146 BC, during the third Punic War, exactly fifty years after another Roman, Flamininus, had declared the freedom of Hellas at the Games held on the very Isthmus itself. Only the temple of Apollo was spared, five columns of which still stand, among the most often photographed pillars in the world. The city was razed, its treasures looted, many of them being shipped off to Rome. The inhabitants were scattered, and the skills of centuries dissipated.

A century later in 44 BC, Julius Caesar refounded Corinth on a grand scale. Thus it comes about that the splendid ruins we behold to-day are an almost theatrical setting for a vital episode in the life of Paul. (The only notable addition of later times was the inevitable embellishment of Hadrian's friend, Herodes Atticus. It was a fountain-house to shelter the famous spring of Pirene, with a nymphaeum attached, and very beautiful it is.) Corinth in Paul's time was the capital of Achaia, that is the province of central and southern Greece, as Thessalonika was of the northern region. The city was approached by a marble-paved road leading from the western port, with colonnades on either side. To the east of the temple, and between it and the road, there was a fine basilica or law-court, the 'royal house' on which the Christians modelled their first churches as soon as they were allowed to build them, instead of meeting, as in Paul's day, in each others' houses. The approach road ended in a gateway which gave access to the agora. So utterly had Mummius destroyed the former city that the agora was simply dumped down on the site of the stadium, the starting-line of which can still be seen, like those at Olympia and Delphi.

On the south side of the agora, the Stoa is the longest colonnade we know of in Greece. It housed a row of shops, in the floor of each of which was a shaft leading down to an underground conduit, so that perishable goods could be suspended in the cool current which it generated as in a refrigerator.

In the middle of the south side of the agora is the raised tribunal, the *Bema*, on which the proconsul would hold court and administer justice. Of all the buildings in Corinth, this is the one most personally connected with Paul, because he was himself cited to attend there. Outside the wall to the north was the theatre, a Roman edifice on a Greek foundation and adapted to Roman beastliness, that is the gladiatorial combats in which the Romans delighted.

It is easy to understand the attractions of so grand and motley a creation. The poet Horace admired what he calls 'twin-sea'd Corinth' so much that he would exclaim 'Not everyone is so lucky as to find his way to Corinth', as though it were the hub of earthly felicity. Well, for some it was. For Paul it was a challenge.

Below:
Epicurus was the son of Athenian colonists on the island of Samos. He taught his doctrines of the independent and untroubled human soul in a secluded garden in Athens for thirty-six years, and his followers would have heard Paul's message with impatience. Epicurus taught at a time when old loyalties to state and religion were being questioned: but his own philosophy was in many aspects a negative one and for many became an excuse for a withdrawal from responsibility.

Below, right:
Corinth lies on the south side of the Isthmus which features so much in both classical legend and classical history. This picture shows the country to the south, the Peloponnese from the height of Acrocorinth.

At the outset of his mission, Paul had two cheering experiences. The first was his meeting with a Jewish-Christian couple called Aquila and Priscilla. Aquila was born in Pontus, on the southern shore of the Black Sea, but had migrated to Rome. They were expelled from that city when, in the year AD 49, the emperor Claudius issued an order that all the Jews were to leave. Such an expulsion was no new thing: on several previous occasions, some going back to the Republic, the Roman government had issued expulsion orders against foreigners or groups of foreigners, who by causing dissension, specially on religious grounds, were a threat to public order. On this occasion, it appears from a note in Suetonius' life of Claudius (25.4) that it was disputes between orthodox Jews, who had long been settled in Rome, and Christian converts, that had caused the touble.

Aquila and his wife had every hope of returning to Rome, as indeed they eventually did (*Romans* XVI. 3). But their sojourn in Corinth was of double advantage for Paul. First, they were able to tell him of the church already established in the capital, which is why he was able to write to them before he ever went there. Secondly, by a happy coincidence Aquila and Priscilla were, like Paul, tentmakers. They took Paul into their house, and he was able to work with them.

The second consolation was the arrival, so anxiously awaited, of Silas and Timothy. They brought wonderful news of the constancy and growth of the church at Thessalonika. They also brought material help. This was of real assistance to Paul, because it meant that he need no longer spend his days at the loom, with only his evenings, and the sabbath, free to pursue his spiritual mission.

The news from Thessalonika was so cheering that Paul decided to write to his flock there. Thus came into being, in or about the year AD 50, the earliest surviving Christian document, Paul's First Letter to the Thessalonians. This might seem surprising to anyone acquainted only with the text of the New Testament, because the Gospels are *placed* first, but not one of them was written until at least the last years of Paul's life. The majority of Paul's letters, if not all, precede them.

We call the Epistles *letters*, but they are more than that, and were so intended to be by Paul. They are more like the 'rescripts' of the emperors. These too were written in the form of letters, as for instance those of Trajan to his friend the Younger Pliny, but they were in fact directions, very often in reply to enquiries—again the Trajan-Pliny comparison holds good—on matters of conduct, belief and practice, so that we still read them with such interest and profit. This being their nature they

were designed as circulars, which is why they have come down to us, instead of just being read and then thrown away. This, *I Thessalonians*, of all Paul's extant letters is constructed on just that plan.

First Paul says how happy and grateful he is for the constancy of the Thessalonian church. He would gladly have come himself to see them, but being unable to leave his present work, he had sent to enquire after them, and now Timothy had brought him this wonderful report. Then comes some stern advice. They are to live modestly, avoiding fornication (then as now a normal pagan pastime), deceit and sloth. They are to mind their own business, and work hard. It would be very wrong to sit back and do nothing, living on the richer brethren, and hoping for the Second Coming: he need not remind them that the day of the Lord will come as a thief in the night, none of us knows when. The final words 'The grace of our Lord Jesus Christ be with you. Amen'. were probably added by Paul in his own hand. The body of the letter would be written, as was the practice in his day, by an amanuensis.

It would take a long time to write. It would be written by a scribe, crouched uncomfortably on the floor, with a pen of reed, or quill on sheets of papyrus. Ricciotti, who made a special study of the subject, reckons (on the basis of similar letters recovered from the sands of Egypt), that the 1,472 words of the original would have required ten sheets of papyrus, and would have taken twenty hours to write.

The fact that ancient letters did take so long to compose explains why so often in Paul's letters we find apparently sudden jumps, differences of style, repetitions. There is no need to talk of 'interpolations', it was just the way they were put together. The leaves were gummed to each other by the margin, thus forming a roll, *volumen* (our

All that remains of the great temple of Apollo at Corinth. The ruins were old even in Paul's day, dating from the time when Corinth was the maritime and commercial centre of Greece with colonies all round the Mediterranean. In the foreground is part of the Stoa, where Paul was summoned to appear before the Roman governor who conducted his court from the raised platform, the *Bema*.

volume). The outside would bear the address, and would be sealed. If it were very bulky, it would be placed in an outer covering. Books, as we understand the word, with pages that turn over, were not then in use. Until recently it was thought that they did not exist until the third century at the earliest; but there is now in the Bodmer Library at Geneva a magnificent copy of the Gospel of St John in book form which must be attributed to the middle of the second.

Paul wrote in the Greek of his day, but his style is that of a cultivated man, not that of the market-place. In modern Greek, the same difference still persists, between the popular and the pure forms of the language, and it still causes acute controversy among Greeks.

In Corinth the by now familiar syndrome was repeated: preaching in the synagogue, conversions, opposition, turning to the Gentiles. In this case, Paul abandoned the synagogue altogether, and took up his abode in the house of a certain Justus, a godfearing man who lived hard by. A notable convert was Crispus, the ruler of the synagogue. He and his family joined the little church, and his example induced many to do likewise. Paul spent eighteen fruitful months, or perhaps a little longer, in Corinth.

During his stay there, a new Proconsul was appointed, named Lucius Junius Gallio, a brother of the philosopher Seneca. Just as the arrival of Aquila and Priscilla gives us a date before which Paul could not have been in Corinth, namely Claudius' expulsion of the Jews from Rome in AD 49, so does the appearance of Gallio, because it is known—perhaps inferred would be a better term—from an inscription found at Delphi in 1905 that Gallio was Proconsul of Achaia in the year 52. But he may have held the office in 51. Bornkamm assumes that he did: Ricciotti admits the possibility. But where the whole chronology is so cloudy, it is valuable to be able to fix one date at least within a year. As Fr Joseph Crehan has pointed out, the basic trouble in determining the dates of Paul's life springs from his use of the term 'fourteen years' in *Galatians* II. 1. He is using a round number— the Jews habitually counted in sevens.

To return to the narrative. The Jews thought that they might be able to persuade the new governor to proceed against Paul. They haled him before the *Bema*, which we can still see, and accused him of being subversive, though without specifying just how—he 'persuaded men to worship God contrary to the law'. Paul was about to answer when Gallio cut both sides short. He appears to have shared his brother's dislike of the Jews. If it were a matter of crime or depravity, he would deal with it, but since it was a question of words and names, and the Jewish law, he would not interfere: they must settle it among themselves, and he ordered his lictors to disperse the crowd. Taking their cue from Gallio, the Greeks now turned on the Jews, assaulted the new ruler of the synagogue, who was called Sosthenes, and thrashed him before the *Bema*. Gallio took no notice. We hear no more of Gallio, but we know from Tacitus that like his brother Seneca, and Paul himself, he fell a victim to Nero, who became emperor in AD 54.

Paul prolonged his stay in Corinth 'a good while' after this incident, and then left the city by the eastern port, Cenchrea, where he shaved his head to solemnize a religious vow. What it was we do not know, but we learn from Josephus that those who suffered from illness (as Paul did) would make a vow, thirty days before the day on which they intended to offer sacrifice, to abstain from wine and to shave their heads. Paul had a firm intention of going to Jerusalem for the Jewish feast of Pentecost or first-fruits, for he was still a pious Jew, and observed the Jewish law as being permissive though no longer obligatory. The ship put in at Ephesus.

The stay there was short, but it included a sabbath on which as was his custom Paul attended synagogue, and his exposition aroused so much interest that the Jews asked him to stay longer. Paul replied that he must go to Jerusalem in order to attend the feast and to fulfill his vow: he would come back to them, he said. The ship in which he was embarked seems to have been a vessel of some importance, since it linked the three Roman provincial capitals, Corinth, Ephesus, and Caesarea in Palestine where Paul landed. He paid his respects to the brethren in Jerusalem, and so returned to Antioch.

Thus ended Paul's second missionary journey, which he had started at the end of the year 49. It was now the spring of 53.

What had Paul achieved? There are two criteria by which his success or failure may be judged. The first is did his infant churches grow up, did they endure as such? The second, which stems from the first, is, were they to prove viable at the bar of history? By both tests, it may be argued that this second journey was the most productive and fruitful of all his travels.

As regards the first test, we are fortunate in possessing some, though by no means all, of the letters he wrote to his 'children'. That to the Thessalonians has already been mentioned. In or about the year 56 when, as we shall see, Paul was living at Ephesus, he had occasion to write to the Corinthians at least three times, and to visit them once again. The church there had been assailed by a variety of problems. Some of these were so ephemeral as to seem almost trivial but as Bornkamm reminds us, '... with the Corinthian epistles more than any others we must always bear in mind the situations and problems with which they deal'. For instance, might a Christian eat meat which was left over from a heathen sacrifice and then found its way to the market? Or was it all right for a Christian to join heathen friends and relations for a meal after a sacrifice?

The issue had been complicated and confused by a group of self-styled 'spirituals' or enthusiasts, who regarded themselves as being on a higher plane than the ordinary Christian, and as such entitled to behave with greater freedom, that is to say licence. Paul cuts through these pretensions. The only real wisdom is the wisdom of love. And so from this long-forgotten controversy there sprang the rhapsody contained in the thirteenth chapter of the first letter, the most beautiful spiritual lyric ever uttered, familiar to myriads unacquainted with its origin (*1 Corinthians* XIII).

Things went from bad to worse in Corinth. The church was torn by sectarian rivalry. 'I am of Paul', 'I am of Apollos'. Apollos was an Alexandrian Jewish Christian whose eloquence and constancy had won him a following among the Corinthian brethren. He was with Paul in Ephesus when *1 Corinthians* was written. Paul rebukes this fissile tendency. 'I have planted, Apollos watered; but God gave the increase' (III. 6).

Still the schism persisted. Paul decided that he must himself revisit Corinth. He was terribly shocked by what he found: the church was in open rebellion against him. He went back to Ephesus, and wrote yet another letter to the Corinthians 'out of much affliction and anguish of heart I wrote unto you with many tears' (*2 Corinthians* II. 4). Titus was despatched with this letter, which combined with Titus' own persuasion had the desired effect. When Paul visited Corinth for the third and last time, he found the church at peace. It was one of his greatest victories.

Delphi, a general view of the theatre and the temple of Apollo. The oldest and most sacred sanctuary of Greece, Delphi has made its contribution to our knowledge of early Christianity. An inscription discovered here in 1905 provides the date of Lucius Junius Gallio's governorship in Corinth; he was the governor who summoned Paul to appear before the *Bema*.

Finally, we read his letter to the Philippians, written some ten years later, from Rome. This has been called the pearl of the epistles. Paul, as we shall see, was to revisit Philippi, and it was here that he would receive the comforting news about Corinth. Paul loved the Philippian church in a very special degree. They never forgot him, nor he them. They were his in the 'fellowship of the Gospel from the first day until now'. He remembers their timely help, when he was so much in need of it in Thessalonika. He writes from prison, but the letter is suffused with joy.

The outstanding achievement of Paul's second journey, taking it all in all, was the evangelization of Greece, of Hellas itself, which had given so much to the spirit of man in times past. Despite all the tribulations that time was to bring, the light of the Christian faith was never to be extinguished in Greece. It was indeed to keep the spirit of Greece alive. And to this day, when Latin is no longer the universal language of the Western Church, Greek remains that of the Holy Orthodox Church, which still endures as one of the greatest monuments to its sole begetter, Paul.

Two views of the canal of which Nero dreamed. The narrow Isthmus of Corinth was an obstacle to shipping, and merchants preferred to carry their cargoes – and often their ships – from one side to the other. Nero's attempt to cut a canal in AD 67 was unsuccessful and another was not made until the nineteenth century; the present canal was opened in 1893. The bird's-eye view looks south-east to the site of ancient Cenchreae and the Saronic Gulf. The picture taken at water-level looks north-west to the Gulf of Corinth and ancient Sicyon.

Far left:
The elaborate edifice erected in the second century AD by Herodes Atticus to contain the spring of Pirene in Corinth. This spring, which attracted people to the city from all over ancient Greece, was believed to have been made by the winged horse, Pegasus, when he stamped his hoofs there.

CHAPTER SEVEN

THE THIRD JOURNEY
EPHESUS

Paul was 'home' again, not in Tarsus, his birthplace 'according to the flesh', but in Antioch, the centre of his missions, the chief church of the Gentiles, whence the light had radiated over parts of two continents. Only parts of them: Paul must see that the little candles he had lighted should throw their beams farther, that the good deeds which grace had wrought by him must shine more brightly in the world. Not for him repose, nor satisfied recollection. He must be off once more. So began what is known as his Third Missionary Journey.

Paul's immediate destination was the group of churches nearest his native land, founded on his first journey, confirmed on his second. It was bound for them that he set out in the spring of the year 53 from the Antioch he was never to see again.

Luke hurries us through the region in half a verse—after all, he has described Paul's work there twice already—so that we do not know exactly what route Paul took 'over all the country of Galatia and Phrygia in order'; (*Acts* XVIII. 23). Holzner has this perspicacious comment: 'Since Luke has nowhere told us of a series of North Galatian Churches, we must understand the South Galatian Churches of Derbe, Lystra, Iconium, Antioch (in Pisidia) and their affiliates. This second diagonal trip across Asia Minor was not, therefore, for the purpose of making new foundations, but to strengthen the Churches already founded and also to arrive at the Ionian coast'.

This makes sense, and Pauline sense: Paul never forgot his children. He loved revisiting them. Holzner adds: 'Those who argue that Paul went to northern Galatia must conclude that he ignored the danger in which the southern Churches were and that he went by forced marches by way of

Cybistra (Eregli) or Tyana, Caesarea, Ancyra, Pessinus and Dorylaeum, across so-called "scorched Phrygia" covered with lava flows, to the Persian highway and so to Ephesus. . . . The trip into northern Galatia would have added about 375 miles, and the entire journey from Tarsus to Ephesus would have totalled 1,060 miles, a journey of about 70 days, since the ancients reckoned 15 miles a day for the ordinary foot-traveller, and 20 miles a day for the imperial courier. Why undergo such hazards, especially as nothing came of it . . . If we add up the mileage of St Paul's three journeys in Asia Minor, we arrive at the following figures: the first journey from Adalia to Derbe and return, 625 miles: the second journey from Tarsus to Troas (without the side trip to Ancyra), 875 miles; the third journey, from Tarsus to Ephesus, 710 miles'. These figures do not include excursions to neighbouring towns here and there. The mere physical achievement is amazing.

Paul now returned to Ephesus, and for a stay of several years. 'He approached it from the north,' says Professor Lloyd, 'coming down from the plateau by the beautiful road which runs down the

Facing page, above:
Paul set out from Antioch on his third missionary journey in the spring of AD 53. The Antioch he left was a great, thriving city of which nothing remains. But he would have travelled on a road not very different from the one shown here.

Below:
Ephesus, looking north. Paul would have approached the city from this side and entered it through the Magnesian Gate. The long, marble-paved street of Ephesus continued all the way to the harbour which made Ephesus one of the greatest ports of the ancient world. A thousand years old even in Paul's day, Ephesus handled the riches of East and West.

Meander river, leaving its source at Apameia (modern Dinar), passing first Colossae and then Hieropolis, now called by the Turks Pamukkale. One reason that has been suggested for Paul not having until now wished to preach in Ephesus is that St John was living there and may have regarded the province of Asia as his own sphere of influence. It is also believed by some that when St John came from Jerusalem to Ephesus in about AD 47, he brought with him the Virgin Mary, who had been especially committed to his charge. One piece of evidence which supports this "Ephesian theory" is that in AD 431, the famous Oecumenical Council of Ephesus was held in a building known as "The Most Holy Church which is called Maria", and which has been identified as the "double basilica", whose ruins were excavated by Austrian archaeologists many years ago.' (It is really two churches of different dates, connected by a rather beautiful little octagonal baptistry.) 'The other discovery relevant to the "Ephesian theory" was the little building on the slopes of Mount Sole-missos above Ephesus, which is to-day known as the "House of the Blessed Virgin", and called by the Turks Panağia Kapulu.'

Professor Lloyd then quotes from Sir William Ramsay's *Pauline Studies* 'the extraordinary (and totally uncontroversial) story of how it came to be found'.

Above, left:
'Diana of the Ephesians.' The ancient fertility goddess of the Eastern Mediterranean was manifest in many forms and under many names and had a firm hold on the imaginations of the people of the Near East, Egypt, Greece and Rome. In Ephesus she was called Artemis but her cult had nothing in common with that of the chaste huntress of the Greeks.

Above:
Ephesus was a city of enormous importance in the Roman world and the emperors were always ready to honour her. A fine temple was raised there in honour of the Philhellene emperor Hadrian, the ruins of which can still be seen. Of the temple of Artemis, one of the wonders of the world, there is no trace other than an enormous water-logged hollow.

Facing page:
Dürer's painting shows John, the young Apostle of the Gospels, with Peter. John is believed to have lived in Ephesus for many years with Mary the mother of Jesus in his care. There is reason to believe that John, after his period of exile on the island of Patmos (by order of the emperor Domitian) returned to Ephesus in his old age to write his Gospel.

'Briefly put,' says Ramsay, 'the story is that early in the last century an uneducated woman in a German convent saw in a vision the place in the hills south of Ephesus, where the Virgin Mary had lived, and described it in detail immediately after she had the vision; that her vision was printed and published in Germany; that after the lapse of fifty years the book came in 1890 into the hands of some Roman Catholics at Smyrna, by whom the trustworthiness of the vision was keenly disputed; that a priest in Smyrna who took a leading part in controverting the authority of the vision made a journey into the mountains in order to prove by actual exploration that no such house existed; and that on the third day of continuous search in the rugged unknown mountains, on Wednesday 19 July 1891 (the Feast of St Martha), he found the house exactly as it was described in the published account of the vision, among surroundings which were also accurately described; and that he returned to Smyrna convinced of the truth against his previous judgement.'

'If,' adds Professor Lloyd, 'after looking at this curious little building with its sacred spring and admiring the view over Ephesus and the Cayster valley from the hilltop above, you read the nun's description again, you cannot help being amazed at the accuracy of her description.'

Pope Paul VI visited Ephesus in 1967, and in the following year High Mass was celebrated in the ruins of the Double Basilica before some thousands of people. Such are the earliest, and the most recent, Christian associations of Ephesus.

During his active ministry Paul made a longer sojourn in Ephesus than in any other city of his own choosing—some two and a half years. (As usual, the chronology is disputed: Holzner and Ricciotti give us the years 54–57, Bornkamm 52–55.) It is interesting to consider why. We may discern three reasons. First, Ephesus was the greatest city of Asia Minor. It was not officially the capital of the Roman province of Asia—Pergamum had always been that—but it was by far the most important city of the province, and the Proconsuls generally resided there. Although it is now some miles from the sea it was in antiquity a great port, through which passed the merchandise of east and west, north and south.

This metropolis of Asia had been more than a thousand years a-growing. Originally, about 1100 BC, it was a settlement of colonists from Athens, attracted by its harbour and its communications with the interior and the orient. Strabo says that on this trade the city grew richer every day: Spain, Sicily, Greece, Egypt and the Black

Sea—all contributed to its opulence. The Ephesus which Paul saw, as he came in through the northern or Magnesian Gate, was the creation of Lysimachus, the humane general and successor of Alexander the Great (d. 323 BC). He encircled the city by the walls we can still see, and many of the astonishingly profuse remains of the city go back to Hellenistic times, though some are Roman, and even post-Pauline. But taken as a whole the site of Ephesus, as we visit it to-day, gives the most vivid and spectacular impression of an early imperial cosmopolis to be found anywhere. No wonder it was an ardent centre of Rome and Caesar-worship.

Even more ardently—and this brings us to the second reason—it was the centre par excellence of the worship of Ephesian Artemis, Diana of the Ephesians as she is called in the Authorised Version. This deity has no more than a name in common with the maiden huntress of Greek mythology. The so-called Artemis of Ephesus was an assimilation of an ancient Asian fertility goddess, the Great Mother who appears in various guises in Asiatic religion. Her image was held to have fallen from Heaven (*Acts* XIX. 35). Her votaries honoured her with orgiastic rites: she was famous far beyond the bounds of Ephesus. Moreover she had two important functions, besides those of her cult.

Her temple possessed the right of asylum: fugitives could seek sanctuary in it. This meant that a number of criminals could find immunity within her precinct. The emperor Tiberius tried to abolish this privilege, but was compelled to yield to the protests of the Ephesians. The second of the temple's ancillary claims to importance was that, like the Temple in Jerusalem, and other shrines, it was a bank. Being sacrosanct, it became the repository of treasure, both private and public. It was the pious custom of the Jews (now imitated by the Christians) to send annual contributions to Jerusalem. It was in Ephesus, in this very temple, that the contributions were assembled. Cicero in the year 61 delivered his famous defence of Flaccus, the governor of Asia, who was accused of preventing the export of the *Aurum Judaicum*, the Temple funds. The matter was settled beyond a doubt, in favour of the Jews, by Augustus' minister Marcus Vipsanius Agrippa and Herod the Great, during their joint tour of the province.

The temple of Artemis itself was accounted one of the seven wonders of the world. Its area was approximately two-thirds that of St Peter's in Rome. The roof was supported by 127 Ionic columns, with finely carved bases. One is now in the British Museum. The temple was razed by Gothic marauders in the year AD 273, and all trace

of it was lost until the nineteenth century. To quote Professor Lloyd once more: 'The ruins of Pre-Roman Ephesus are now buried beneath about twenty feet of alluvial soil: and this explains among other things the huge water-logged hollow which is all there is to be seen at the site of the famous Artemisium or "Temple of Diana". You may know that, starting in 1869 the British railway engineer, J. T. Wood, went on trenching for six years before he eventually lighted on the ruins of the Hellenistic temple' (and also parts of an earlier one) 'twenty feet below the present surface. One has seen pictures of him, in his frock coat and stove-pipe hat which he always wore, resting his elbow on a sculptured column-drum, unaware poor fellow that his excavations had stopped short of the fabulous foundation-deposit which was found by D. G. Hogarth thirty years later—many hundreds of gold or electrum objects with statues of Artemis in bronze and ivory'.

The third reason why Ephesus attracted Paul is simply the combination of the first two: Ephesus was a challenge, unprecedented and not to be shrunk from.

Paul was not the first to evangelize Ephesus. Apollos, already mentioned, had worked there. He was now in Corinth but Paul of course met his disciples. He found that Apollos, devout man though he was, had preached only 'unto John's baptism': not the Gospel of Jesus of Nazareth to which it was, in Paul's view, only a preliminary.

The little building where Mary is believed to have passed the last years of her life. There is an authenticated account of a woman living in a German convent who, in 1840, had a vision which showed her the place where Mary had lived. Her vision was not investigated for fifty years; then a priest from Smyrna found the house exactly where it was described in the vision on Mount Solemissos, above Ephesus.

Aquila and Priscilla had heard him preaching in the synagogue. He was eloquent, and very well versed in the scriptures, as was to be expected of a Jew from Alexandria, the city of the great Jewish philosopher and exegete Philo. So Aquila and Priscilla 'expounded unto him the way of God more perfectly'. Paul soon discovered that these 'near-Christians' had not even heard of the Holy Spirit. There were about a dozen of them. Paul baptized them in the name of Christ, and then confirmed them by laying his hands on them. To Paul it was the Holy Spirit who was his sole guide, and so that same Spirit must be the guide of his converts. It appears from the narrative in *Acts* that for them, too, the consciousness that they had received this charisma was a thrilling experience: we are told (XIX. 6) that they 'spake with tongues and prophesied', that is, they underwent a Pentecostal renewal.

By his action in regard to these disciples of the 'anteroom', as Holzner aptly calls them, Paul had ensured that the church in Ephesus should be one, and that it would be what we should now call catholic and apostolic. He could thus go ahead with his mission. For three months he proclaimed the kingdom of God in the synagogue. Then, as usual, his success produced the inevitable opposition. He left the synagogue, and moved into a hall in the school of a certain Tyrannus, who seems from his name to have been a Greek teacher of rhetoric (for such the word 'school' Greek *Skholé*, literally 'leisure', denotes, studies being the privilege of the leisured.) One of the our earliest and most important manuscripts, the sixth century *Bezae*, now at Cambridge, tells us the hours during which Paul had the use of the hall, from the equivalent of our eleven in the forenoon until four. This would have suited both Tyrannus and Paul. The ancients, both Greek and Roman, started the day with the dawn, as many Mediterranean folk still do. Tyrannus would lecture during the first hours of the day, while Paul was busy at the loom and no doubt planning his discourse, which he then proceeded to deliver when Tyrannus vacated the hall.

For two years Paul maintained his strenuous régime. He found time to write to his friends in Galatia, in Corinth, in Philippi. He received visitors not only from all over the province with its 500 towns, many of which he must have visited (*Acts* XIX. 10), but from Greece as well; Gaius and Aristarchus from Macedonia, Secundus from Thessalonika, Sopater from Berea among them. The church grew, not only in Ephesus but throughout Asia, so much so that when a generation or so later St John wrote his Apocalypse on the island of Patmos, he addressed it not to Ephesus only, but to the Seven Churches now established (though by no means all equally firmly) in the province, namely, Ephesus, Smyrna, Pergamum, Thyatira, Sardis, Philadelphia and Laodicea. Meanwhile Paul's personal charisma had become so famous that he was credited with miraculous powers and clothes which had been in contact with his body (as later with *myrrhoblutes*) were held to be efficacious in curing the sick.

False thaumaturges were quick to exploit Paul's success. It was, they probably reckoned, a soft touch. In a world riddled with superstition as the Roman world was, from top to bottom, if someone like Paul could produce 'strong medicine', why not use it? There was a Jew called Sceva, with seven sons, who made up a lucrative group of conjurers. Two of them decided to try the new charm on a possessed man. 'We adjure you' (the evil spirit) 'by Jesus whom Paul preacheth'. But everything went wrong. The afflicted man (*Acts* XIX. 15) gave them the chilling answer: 'Jesus I know, and Paul I know; but who are ye?' Then he leaped on them and thrashed them 'so that they fled out of that house naked and wounded'.

This vindication of Paul as the paramount practitioner set off a chain-reaction. First of all, many believers were stung into confessing that they too had meddled in superstitious practices (who in Ephesus had not?), which they now abjured for good. Others followed their example, even professional magicians. Ephesus had its own particular brand of magical prescription, known as *Ephesia grammata*, charms written in a sort of gibberish. Statues of the Great Goddess are adorned with them. These charms could be used as love-philtres, talismans or to promote success in business. They had a very wide vogue. Their owners now collected them, together with ordinary manuals of magic, and burned them publicly. (Such holocausts of forbidden books occurred in the pagan world: Livy mentions one (XL. 29). Even as late as the fourth century AD, so Ammianus tells us, a similar bonfire took place). The value of the writings burned at Ephesus amounted to the huge sum of 50,000 silver drachmae, about £3,000.

Paul now had more reason than ever to feel satisfied with his labours in Ephesus, and with the abundant harvest they had produced. He therefore planned to revisit his churches in northern and southern Greece, then to return to Jerusalem and finally 'I must also see Rome' (*Acts* XIX. 21). That he had long contemplated such a visit is clear from *Romans* XV. 24, written a little later during Paul's last visit to Corinth. To prepare the way for his

arrival in Greece, he sent ahead Timothy and Erastus. His plans for an orderly departure, after due dispositions made, were suddenly and rudely upset by a riot, the description of which is one of Luke's most vivid pictures.

There was in Ephesus a man called Demetrius, who appears to have been the president of the guild of silversmiths. The Romans were extremely chary of allowing any clubs or guilds to be formed (the emperor Trajan would even forbid the enrolling of a fire brigade in Bithynia), because they feared they might be used for political ends or to cause disturbances; but they did sometimes permit *bona fide* trade associations. It is important to bear this in mind when considering what now occurred in Ephesus.

Demetrius called his workmen together and harangued them. They earned their living, he reminded them, by making little silver shrines of Artemis, for pilgrims to buy as souvenirs of their visits. But look what had happened: this man Paul, not only in Ephesus but almost throughout the whole province, had perverted thousands, telling them that hand-made gods had no real existence. The result was doubly harmful. First, if people stopped buying their products, what would happen to them? Secondly, the great temple itself would be despised and that would be the end of Ephesus and its world-wide fame.

When the artisans heard this they became extremely angry and excited. They rushed through the streets, shouting out their slogan: 'Great is Diana of the Ephesians!' Not finding Paul himself they siezed two of his travelling companions, Gaius and Aristarchus, both Macedonians, and converged on the one place suitable for an assembly, the theatre. (It is more than probable that it was these two men who gave Luke the material for his narrative.)

The theatre or stadium was the one place under the empire where a large number of people could congregate. That mere fact made it a source of disquiet to Rome's rulers. Even the emperor Hadrian lost his nerve once when attending the races. Marcus Aurelius, the calm philosopher, hated having to be present in the Colosseum. The theatre at Ephesus—it is still there—held 24,000 spectators, and owing to the very steep rake of the seating, they must have seemed to be literally 'on top' of anyone in the orchestra or on the stage.

As soon as Paul heard what had happened he wanted to go to the theatre himself; but his disciples held him back. So did his friends among the City Council, Asiarchs, as they were rather grandly called, their chief function being to superintend the cult of Rome and Caesar, of which as already noted Ephesus was a centre. As usual, Paul had made allies of authority, once they realized who he was. As we shall see, he was to do so on more than one later occasion. Meanwhile the riotous assembly went on: everybody was shouting at once, and only a few knew what is was all about. At this juncture, the Jews, thinking that the disorder was aimed at them, put forward one of their community called Alexander. He held up his hand, and tried to begin a speech in which he intended to show that the Jewish community had nothing to do with the silversmiths' cause for alarm. When the mob recognized him as being a Jew they howled him down, and, by now having become hysterical as an Oriental mob so easily does, simply went on chanting 'Great is Diana of the Ephesians!' for another two hours.

At this point the town clerk, reckoning that the rioters would be physically exhausted, intervened. He managed to calm them down, and then addressed them with great tact. 'Ye men of Ephesus,' he said, 'What man is there that knoweth not how that the city of the Ephesians is a worshipper of the great goddess Diana, and of the image which fell down from Jupiter? Seeing then that these things cannot be spoken against, ye ought to be quiet, and to do nothing rashly. For ye have brought hither these men, which are neither robbers of churches, nor yet blasphemers of your goddess. Wherefore if Demetrius, and the craftsmen which are with him, have a matter against any man, the law is open, and there are [proconsuls]: let them [bring charges against] one another. But if ye enquire any thing concerning other matters, it shall be determined in a lawful assembly. For we are in danger to be called in question for this day's uproar, there being no cause whereby we may give an account of this concourse.' (*Acts* XIX. 35–40).

That clinched the argument. The town clerk had very neatly turned the tables on the mob: it was they, not their opponents, who would be in trouble. He told them to disperse, which they accordingly did.

Paul had been intending to leave Ephesus: now it was imperative that he should do so. He summoned his disciples, embraced them, and set off down the great columned way that led to the harbour, there to embark for Greece.

This strangely anachronistic painting by Eustache le Sueur (seventeenth century) was meant to depict the episode at Ephesus described in *Acts* XIX. 19. The books are of a kind the ancients never knew, and the burning was not presided over by Paul.

CHAPTER EIGHT

THE THIRD JOURNEY
HELLAS REVISITED

It was now spring again, when the seas were once more open for navigation. Paul was bent on revisiting his Greek churches. He was accompanied by Timothy, Gaius and Aristarchus, Secundus, Tychicus and Trophimus. They made for Troas. Following the practice of the time they sailed up the coast, keeping land in sight wherever possible and generally landing at dusk. In those pre-compass days, it was not always possible to get a bearing after dark, for the night sky might be overcast. At Troas, a certain Carpus was their host. Paul had been in Troas seven years before. Then, the Spirit had forbidden him to preach; now (*2 Corinthians* II. 12) 'a door was opened unto me'.

But he was anxious to reach Macedonia and did not stay long: he wanted Titus' report on Corinth. So they met at Philippi, where Paul also appears to have been reunited with Luke, after some years separation. Titus' report was full of consolation, for reasons which are indicated in Paul's second letter to the Corinthians, or rather in the fragments of several letters which form that epistle.

'For, when we were come into Macedonia, our flesh had no rest, but we were troubled on every side; without were fightings, within were fears. Nevertheless God, that comforteth those that are cast down, comforted us by the coming of Titus; and not by his coming only, but by the consolation wherewith he was comforted in you, when he told us of your earnest desire, your mourning, your fervent mind toward me; so I rejoiced the more.' (*2 Corinthians* VII. 5–7). Paul goes on to say he was sorry he had written to them as he had; but it had worked out well in the end, because it had made them sorry, too. Now all of them, including Paul, could be glad. And he asks them to follow the example of the Macedonians and contribute to his relief fund for the poor brethren in Jerusalem.

It appears from *Romans* XV. 19 that Paul made a journey into Illyricum, modern Dalmatia. This province lay to the north of the Via Egnatia. It had been turbulent in quite recent times. Its inhabitants were to retain their warlike qualities until the end of the empire, and some of Rome's best soldier-emperors would be Illyrians. Altogether, Paul spent three months in northern Greece. When the winter of the year 57 (Bornkamm would put it a year earlier) set in Paul had once more, and for the last time, visited Corinth; a Corinth at peace with a growing church, the result of Paul's labours, perseverance and above all love. Was it not to this flock that his great hymn of Love had been addressed?

'The winter was past.' (Holzner reminds us.) 'On March 5, Rome had solemnly opened the sailing season with religious ceremonies and the launching of the *navigium Isidis*, the Egyptian guardian of the sea.' Paul now planned to go to Jerusalem and then to Rome. To Jerusalem because he had to deliver the relief-fund to the brethren there; but there must have been in his mind the thought that a Jerusalem-Rome axis, as we might put it now-adays, was the essential substructure for a universal church such as he now envisaged. Normally, Paul would have taken ship at Cenchreae, and thence by the inter-island route, after touching the south coast of Asia, would have made for Caesarea, as he had done on his second journey. But just as he was about to set out, he was warned of a plot against his life, formed by Jewish antagonists (*Acts* XX. 3). As we shall shortly see, the Jewish world

The Nea Moni monastery on the island of Chios. Chios, like Lesbos, was one of the islands where Paul's ship called on his journey back to Jerusalem. Chios is noted for its monasteries, most of which occupy a beautiful setting.

was in a state of feverish unrest and resentment against its Roman overlords. Inevitably, therefore, Paul, born a Jew but now a Roman citizen, must have appeared as a renegade, especially to devout orthodox Jews such as would now be thronging the shipping-lanes en route for the Passover in Jerusalem.

Paul's companions, perhaps to act as decoys, made straight for Troas while Paul and Luke went back into Macedonia. It was at Philippi that Passover was celebrated. Then they embarked, and reached Troas, after a voyage of five days (which means they made about thirty miles a day only) compared with the two days which the voyage in the opposite direction had taken. At Troas Paul and Luke found the rest of the company and, understandably tired after their trying voyage, decided to stay there a week.

It was already the custom of the Christians to meet together for commemorative worship on the 'first day of the week', the day of the Resurrection, our Sunday; and also, as we learn from (1 Corinthians XVI. 2) to collect alms, just as is done in church to-day. At Troas, the first day fell on the eve of the apostles' departure, so that it had a special significance for both them and their flock. Before proceeding to the liturgical breaking of bread—it took place, as on the occasion of its original institution by Jesus, in an upper room— Paul started to preach. He went on so long that a young man called Eutychus, for whom the day had not been as it now is a day of rest, feeling drowsy, went and sat on an open window-ledge. Even there, the heat of many lights, of the crowded congregation, was so oppressive that, as Paul went on and on, he fell into a deep sleep. So deep that he fell out of the window, and crashed into the street three storeys below. He was taken up for dead. Paul, with astounding *sang-froid*, administered the kiss of life and told the congregation not to worry: 'Trouble not yourselves; for his life is in him'. Then he went upstairs again, went on with the breaking of the bread, and then delivered another sermon which lasted until after midnight. This incident may appear trivial, and it is not without its humorous side; but regarded rightly it shows

Below:
The harbour of Mytilene on the island of Lesbos.

Facing page:
A Hellenistic gold platter showing the goddess Cybele and her consort Attis in a chariot drawn by lions, with the symbols of the goddess's cult. In Paul's day there was a famous shrine to Cybele on the island of Chios.

yet again Paul's amazing power of commanding a situation, restoring tranquility, and doing what he had intended to do.

Next morning, Paul's companions left Troas (Eutychus was there to see them off), and coasted down to Assos, on the other side of the headland. Assos still retains its rock-built citadel, and much of its girdle of magnificent battlements, amid a gentle agricultural countryside. Paul made the journey on foot and joined them there; the group continued down the coast. To quote Professor Lloyd once more: 'Paul's return journey is carefully described by Luke, who being a Greek, had a lively interest in anything to do with the sea. . . . One almost envies the missionaries these summer journeys by boat between the Aegean coast and the islands—with their views of little harbour towns and, behind them, the shadows of clouds chasing one another across the blue mountainsides. Even Herodotus described these parts of the Aegean as "places more favoured by skies and seasons than any country known to us"'.

Next day the travellers came to Mytilene, the great harbour of the island of Lesbos, the home of the poets Alcaeus and Sappho. Mytilene was a port of great strategic value, being the first haven on the Asian side below the Dardanelles. Agrippa had used it, and so had Herod the Great when on his way to join his Roman friend with an auxiliary squadron. The island is dominated by the ruins of a fortress built partly by the Genoese, partly by the Turks, but the island is now once more united to Greece. Then on to the island of Chios, rich in flowers and fruits, Homer's most probable birthplace, and still a haunt of Christian monastics who dwell in lovely abodes. In the days of Paul, Chios was noted among other things for its shrine of Cybele, the great goddess. He was to change all that.

They sailed past Ephesus; Paul dare not set foot again in that rowdy metropolis where, as he afterwards put it, he had 'fought with wild beasts'. The next day they made Samos, only a mile off the Asian shore, and beneath Mount Mycale, where of old the Ionian Council had assembled.

Human habitation on Samos was very old. The Samians were typical Ionians, enterprising colonists—they founded settlements as far afield as Egypt—keen engineers, shipbuilders, architects. They created not only the first colonnaded temple known to us, in the eighth century BC; but were also determined to raise the largest, which was to be 365 feet by 179 feet. This huge task was too

much even for the Samians and it was never completed. The underground aqueduct, bored beneath a mountain; the harbour mole: these rivalled the great temple in the days of Polycrates (*c.* 530 BC). Pythagoras was a Samian, and Herodotus spent some time there. The island was indeed the very mirror of Ionian perfection. Here, if anywhere, it is possible to feel the continuity of the human spirit, of the perennial philosophy—here and in Miletus, where Paul arrived the following day.

Of all the cities of Ionia, Miletus to-day extends the most endearing welcome. It is not yet converted (like Pergamum, Ephesus or Perge) into an 'attraction', caged in wire, and pock-marked with booths and kiosks. Like so many other cities of ancient Asia, it has lost its once busy harbours through silting. There were four—from which Milesian colonists and traders carried her arts and commerce to lands as far distant as Egypt and the Crimea. Minoans, Mycenaeans, Carians followed each other into the fertile promontory. A Milesian contingent fought by Priam's side at Troy. Then came the Attic immigrants, who made Miletus the most famous of all the twelve cities of Ionia. One great Milesian, Hippodamus, has already been

Samos, a view from the East Cape looking across to the foothills of Mount Mycale. The people of this beautiful Aegean island were among the most enterprising of the Ionian world.

Facing page, above:
Miletus, like so many of the formerly prosperous seaports of Ionia, has fallen victim to the tragic erosion of the hinterland which has led to vast quantities of silt being deposited in the harbour mouth, thus choking it to death. The once lovely city is overgrown but the remains provide the visitor with a remarkably strong suggestion of the city which was another of Paul's resting places.

Below:
The excavation of an early Christian basilica on the western shore of Kos. The island was the birthplace of Hippocrates, the father of medical science, and would have been of great interest to Luke, the 'beloved physician'. As it was, the little group had little time to spare on the island.

mentioned. But before him Miletus had been the cradle of philosophers; of Thales, the first man to foretell an eclipse; of Anaximander and Anaximenes. Like Paul, these men were bent on seeking truth for, like Paul, they knew that truth would set them free.

Much of the great city that greeted Paul may still be contemplated by the modern pilgrim: the theatre, like those at Ephesus and elsewhere built by Greeks, and adapted by Romans for their barbarous exhibitions of carnage; the agoras, the council-house, the stadium, the encircling ramparts. Musing in this silent city on a spring day, when the white-plumed egrets wheel above the golden-hued iris which enamels the grey ruins, it is easy to recall that never-ending quest in which so many took part, from Thales to Paul, in this very town.

Miletus was now to be the setting for a scene as pathetic as had ever been witnessed in the city's theatre, one which was to have more abiding effect than the most poignant Greek drama. Paul sent two of his assistants up the Meander valley, at the mouth of which Miletus stands, to Ephesus, in order to summon the elders of the church. Even

if he could not revisit Ephesus he was most desirous of bidding them an affectionate farewell. When they arrived Paul delivered his valedictory address. Luke has preserved a record of the speech, and it is worth remarking, in view of the now rather outmoded criticism that the speeches in the works both of Thucydides and Luke—in both they occupy about a quarter of the whole work—are simply 'set pieces' inserted by the author, that the language in this discourse is strikingly similar to that of Paul's own letters. It is given in *Acts* xx. 18–35.

It was a sad parting, full of foreboding not only for himself but for his children who, he sorrowfully warns them, will see his face no more. For himself, he goes 'bound in spirit to Jerusalem, not knowing the things that shall befall me there: save that the Holy Ghost witnesseth in every city, saying that bonds and afflictions abide me'. After commending them all to God, and again emphasizing that he had laboured for no material gain, but had earned his bread with his own hands, he ends: 'I have shewed you all things, how that so labouring ye ought to support the weak, and to remember the words of the Lord Jesus, how he said, "It is more blessed to give than to receive".' This last is a 'saying' of Jesus, not recorded in any of the Gospels. 'And when he had thus spoken, he kneeled down, and prayed with them all. And they all wept sore, and fell on Paul's neck, and kissed him, sorrowing most of all for the words which he spake, that they should see his face no more. And they accompanied him unto the ship.'

Still coasting, the ship next made for Kos, the charming island which faces Halicarnassus (Bodrum) on the mainland. Luke must have found it of particular and personal interest, for Kos is the birthplace of Hippocrates, the father of medicine, that is of medical science, who was born there *c.* 460 BC. The island also possessed an Asklepieion, or precinct of Asklepios, the mythical god of healing, in which treatment was largely psychological, suggestion and hypnosis playing a large part (and to judge from the remains of this and other similar precincts at Pergamum and Epidaurus a successful one) in the therapy. Paul, whose treatment of psychopathic cases has already been exemplified in his dealings with 'magicians' and the 'possessed' must also have found this a congenial port of call. Kos bears testimony to Paul's own faith, for down by the harbour is a well-preserved fortress of the Knights of Saint John. Next day they came to Rhodes, which is even more extensively dominated by the buildings of the Order, of which it was the home from soon after the time when they were

Hippocrates of Kos. A bust in the Capitoline Museum, Rome.

Right:
The site of the Aesklepieion of Pergamum, which lies near the *skene* wall of the great theatre. The Aesklepieions some of which were very famous in the ancient world, were shrines and healing centres dedicated to the Greek god of medicine, Apollo's son Asklepios. It is interesting to speculate on Luke's acquaintance with them.

expelled from Palestine, that is from 1310 until 1522, when Rhodes fell to the Turks.

In Paul's day Rhodes was famous as a centre of philosophers and orators. It had a long and splendid history behind it. Three cities, Lindos, Ialysos and Kamiros, of the first and last of which picturesque vestiges still greet the traveller, sent forth bands of colonists in the usual early Greek pattern to Sicily, the Lipari islands, even to north-east Spain. Towards the end of the Peloponnesian War the Rhodians revolted from their Athenian overlords and built their new capital city, Rhodes, with its twin harbours and its grid-plan layout. Alexander the Great captured it, and thus began three centuries of prosperity. Trade increased, and the Rhodian code was accepted as international maritime law. Unfortunately, in the struggle between Caesar and Pompey, Rhodes backed Pompey (who had rid the sea of pirates in 67 BC) and so felt the victor's wrath.

But such was her vigour that her sculptors, painters, men of letters and above all her orators and philosophers maintained her prestige. Cassius, Cicero himself, studied oratory under Rhodian masters. The emperor Tiberius, when as heir-designate of Augustus he retired from Rome to avoid unpleasantness with his mother and his stepfather, spent eight years in Rhodes, living as a Greek. As in Kos, it is the manifold presence of the Christian knights of St John of Jerusalem that nowadays impresses us, specially the great hospital, because the ministry of Luke has always animated the Christian Church. It was in Rhodes that Paul said his last farewell to Hellas.

The vessel sailed for Patara, now a forlorn petty township. The little bay which gave shelter to ships in antiquity is like so many others completely silted up. Only the ruins of a theatre, seventy metres in diameter, and a triple-arched monumental gateway speak of its past glories; but in Paul's day it was an important haven and entrepôt. Its principal sanctuary was a famous temple of the Lycian Apollo, which at one time rivalled Delphi itself in riches and authority. Here, the voyagers left their little coaster, and embarked in a ship bound for Syria. Sailing south-east, they skirted the south coast of Cyprus, and made for Tyre where the ship was to unload. And no wonder: Tyre was and had long been one of the great emporia of the Levant, one of the chief cities of the Phoenicians, the traders *par excellence* of the era; her merchant fleet was incomparable. As we have seen, Zeno himself was the son of a Phoenician trader. Its opulence in the sixth century BC has been described for us by Ezekiel, in one of the most majestically poetical dooms in all literature (*Ezekiel* XXVII).

'They have made all thy ship boards of fir trees of Senir:' (Mount Hermon) 'they have taken cedars from Lebanon to make masts for thee. Of the oaks of Bashan have they made thine oars; the company of the Ashurites' (Assyrians) 'have made thy benches of ivory, brought out of the isles of Chittim' (Hellas). 'Fine linen with broidered work from Egypt was that which thou spreadest forth to be thy sail; blue and purple from the isles of Elishah' (Achaia) 'was that which covered thee. The inhabitants of Zidon and Arvad' (Ruad, off Tripoli) 'were thy mariners.' Men of every nation came to Tyre, even from afar as Persia, to enlist as mercenaries: '. . . they hanged the shield and helmet in thee; they set forth thy comeliness'.

This navy and army protected and promoted commerce on a grand scale; trade in all sorts of metals from iron to gold, horses, slaves, textiles

and precious stones. Above all, there was the Tyrian dye, which produced the finest purple cloth available. All this was to perish, says Ezekiel, and Tyre was to become 'a place to spread nets upon', which it now literally is. It was Alexander the Great that put an end to Tyre's fabulous pre-eminence. The city was built on an island; but during a famous and protracted siege, Alexander built a causeway, still existing, along which his troops and engines moved inexorably to capture the town. During the rule of Alexander's successors, the Seleucids, Tyre recovered much of its prosperity, and by the days of Paul its lofty buildings rivalled those of Rome. Here in Tyre, Paul heard the latest news from Jerusalem. It was bad. During the seven days that Paul spent in Tyre the disciples begged him not to venture into the Holy City.

To grasp the present state of affairs, we must refer to the death of King Agrippa I (Herod Agrippa). Claudius would have liked to send out as his successor Agrippa's son, called by the same name, who was then living with him in Rome. But the lad was only seventeen, and the cabal of freedmen led by Pallas, Narcissus and Felix had no intention of letting such a useful appointment slip through their fingers if they could help it. They persuaded the emperor that the situation in Palestine needed firm handling, and so once again Judaea became a procuratorial province. The indignation of the Jews may be imagined. Of the first two procurators, each of whom held office for two years, the Jewish historian Josephus says that they gave no affront to the customs of the country, and maintained peace (*Wars* II. 220, *Antiquities* XIX. 103). Under the third, Ventidius Cumanus, who started his four year tenure in 48, the troubles began which were to lead to the ruin of the Jews.

The third procurator's troops were very unwisely, indeed insultingly, recruited from among the pagans of Caesarea and Sebaste. During Passover, when Jerusalem was thronged with pilgrims, one of these soldiers by making an obscene gesture

A head of Silenus from Rhodes. Carved from porphyry, it dates from the second century BC. Rhodes enjoyed great prosperity in the Greek world, it was a centre of capital and exchange and the Rhodian fleet was large and efficient. Much of this prosperity faded under the Romans, who proclaimed Delos a rival free port to punish the Rhodians for their lack of firm support in the third Macedonian war. But the island was a much-loved cultural centre in Paul's time. Silenus was one of the nature spirits of Greek religion, often portrayed as a shaggy father figure.

while on duty in the Temple precinct started a riot. The troops were called out and thousands were crushed to death in the ensuing panic. Another soldier desecrated a scroll of the Law. He was publicly executed. Next, the Samaritans attacked a group of Galileans who were bound for a feast in Jerusalem, and killed a number of them. Cumanus took no action. The Jews of Jerusalem retaliated, and Cumanus had to disperse them with a troop of horse. The whole country was given over to robbery, assault and bloodshed.

The Samaritans made haste to appeal to the new governor of Syria, Ummidius Quadratus— closely followed by the Jews with an appeal of their own. Ummidius held his first enquiry in Tyre itself then went down to Caesarea to investigate matters on the spot. After ordering the crucifixion and beheading of a number of Jewish ringleaders he sent off two former high priests, with two other Jewish notables and the Samaritan leaders, to Claudius. Cumanus and his chief of staff were also despatched to Rome.

When the affair came before Claudius, his freedmen naturally backed Cumanus and the Samaritans; but young Agrippa II prevailed on behalf of his brother Jews. Three Samaritans were executed, Cumanus was banished, and his chief of staff was

returned to Jerusalem where he was beheaded.

To succeed Cumanus the emperor, shortly before his death in AD 54, appointed Antonius Felix. This Felix was a freedman of Antonia, the emperor's mother, whence the name Antonius instead of Claudius, and brother of the emperor's own freedman, Pallas. Tacitus (*History* v. 9) says of Felix that he exercised the authority of a king with the mind of a slave, relying on his brother's influence at court. Suetonius also (*Claudius* 28) tells us of the unheard-of rise to riches and power of this groundling, and says he became the husband of three queens. The first was a grand-daughter of Antony and Cleopatra, by which union Felix actually became related to the emperor himself. The second was Drusilla, sister of Agrippa II. She was already married to Aziz, King of Emesa (Homs), but she now deserted him and went to live in adultery with Felix. (Who his third queen was we do not know.)

Claudius died in the autumn of 54, to be succeeded by Nero, his wife Agrippina's nephew by her first husband. Agrippina's lover was Pallas, the brother of Felix, who naturally now felt himself to be in a stronger position than ever. Sure of the imperial favour, Felix set about the eradication of the brigands. He captured one leader by treachery

and sent him off to Rome in chains. The rank and file were hunted down and summarily crucified. It was becoming dangerous now to make daylight assaults, so the terrorists adopted the curved knife, somewhat like a sickle, which had been used by Illyrian pirates, the Latin name for which was *sica* (sickle). Those who used it were known as *sicarii*. As early as 81 BC Rome had had to legislate against them. The knife could so easily be hidden in the clothes: one swift blow, and the victim was dead, the assassin mixing undetected with the by-standers.

Felix soon fell out with the very man, an ex-high priest, to whose intervention with Claudius he owed his appointment. He had him murdered. The reign of terror began; no one felt safe. And it was the procurator, the very man who should have preserved law and order, who had unleashed the violence. The terrified people fell an easy prey to deceivers of every kind. False prophets and miracle-workers exploited the general unrest; claiming divine inspiration, they lured multitudes into the desert, promising signs and wonders and the coming of freedom. Felix sent horse and foot soldiers to break up the movement. Many were arrested, many others killed.

The most formidable of these impostors was an

Above:
Nero (left) and Agrippina (right). Agrippina was the fourth wife and niece of the emperor Claudius: Nero was her son by her first husband. Ambitious and greedy, Agrippina secured the succession for Nero when Claudius married her. It is generally believed that she poisoned Claudius in AD 54. She wielded almost equal power with Nero during the early part of his reign but he determined to be rid of her authority and had her murdered in AD 59. The likenesses are from coins minted at Antioch in AD 56.

Left:
The terrace of Herod's temple at Sebaste, the city he built on the site of the ancient Samaria.

Egyptian, the same as is mentioned in *Acts* XXI. 38. He summoned the populace of Jerusalem to assemble on the Mount of Olives, whence he declared he would lead them into the citadel of Jerusalem—the walls having crumbled—as those of Jericho had done for Joshua. Felix broke up the assembly, but the Egyptian escaped, which is why he comes into the story of Paul. Meanwhile the murder and the burning of great estates continued. The lawless were paramount. Any village that refused to support them was razed to the ground.

It was against this sombre and seething back-ground that the drama of Paul's last appearance in the Holy Land was to be played out.

CHAPTER NINE

RETURN TO JERUSALEM

Paul learned all about this sad state of affairs from the brethren at Tyre; the news confirmed his own worst forebodings, and yet he knew that he must press on. He and his companions sailed down the coast to Ptolemais, where a beautiful little town now shines at the northern end of the bay above Mount Carmel. In ancient days the town was called Ptolemais after the Egyptian ruler Ptolemy, who captured it when after the death of Alexander the Great in 323 BC he made himself master of Egypt and Palestine. Its original semitic name was Akko, and in a latinized form it reverted to it in the days of the Crusaders of whom it still retains many beautiful memorials. They called it St Jean d'Acre, and it was their last foothold in the Holy Land. They were expelled from it in 1291. It was before the walls of Acre that Admiral Sydney Smith defeated Napoleon in 1799. Later, in exile, Napoleon declared that his star had set at Acre.

In Paul's day, Ptolemais was a Roman colony, inhabited by veterans. After one day spent with the little church there, Paul and his company set out for Caesarea. There, in the largely Gentile Roman capital, Paul could feel comparatively secure. He and his companions lodged with Philip, the evangelist, and one of the original seven deacons. He was an old and tried friend, one of the true pioneers of the Faith. He had four unmarried daughters, who also 'prophesied', that is they helped in spreading knowledge of the Way.

While the party were at Caesarea—and they stayed there some time—Agabus, presumably the same seer as had foretold the famine to the disciples at Antioch, came down from Jerusalem. He now foretold bane for Paul. Like the Hebrew prophets of old, he performed a symbolical act. He took Paul's girdle, and bound with it his own hands and feet, and said: 'Thus saith the Holy Ghost, So shall the Jews at Jerusalem bind the man that owneth this girdle, and shall deliver him into the hands of the Gentiles'. When Paul's companions heard this, from so tried a seer, they all, including Luke and the brethren in Caesarea, implored him not to go up to Jerusalem. To which Paul answered: 'What mean ye to weep and to break mine heart? for I am ready not to be bound only, but also to die at Jerusalem for the name of the Lord Jesus'. Clearly Paul was not to be deterred, so 'The will of the Lord be done', they all said (*Acts* XXI. 10–14).

The whole party now prepared to go up to Jerusalem. The danger facing Paul was indeed formidable. In the present sensitive atmosphere, he would hardly be *persona grata*. As a Roman citizen, he would appear to every patriotic Jew as a 'Romanizer', a collaborator with the oppressor. To the Judaeo-Christian church he was a Hellenizer, a man who not only consorted with Gentiles but taught Jews to desert their Law. The fact that Paul had with him a collection taken up from the Gentiles for the benefit of the Jerusalem community only added to their embarrassment: it could so easily be regarded as hush-money, as a bribe in fact.

Paul understood this perfectly well. He was the last man to want to cause difficulties to anyone, certainly not to his own relations. It was therefore determined that instead of staying with his sister or her son, Paul should lodge with a Cypriot, a Christian of long standing called Mnason who by good fortune was then in Caesarea on his way to the Holy City. Thus the whole company, which now included some of the brethren from Caesarea

The Crusaders' fort at Acre. In Paul's time the city was called Ptolemais, and it was here that he disembarked on his last journey to Jerusalem.

itself, set off for Jerusalem.

The first meeting with the brethren in Jerusalem was cordial. Next day, an appointment was made for the newly-arrived group, including Luke, to wait on the venerable James and his little chapter. After saluting them as loyalty and affection demanded, Paul frankly discoursed to them of the wonderful things which God had wrought through his ministry among the Gentiles. He spoke about them precisely and in detail. James and the elders could not but welcome this report; but at the same time they were constrained to point out to Paul that there were *Jews*, many thousands of them, who while adhering to the Faith were at the same time 'zealous of the Law'. These orthodox brethren had been told that Paul has been going about to persuade the Jews of the Diaspora (the Dispersion), to forsake the Mosaic law and tradition; in fact to cease being Jews altogether, to apostatize. What therefore should be done? The news of Paul's arrival was bound to spread, and a

movement hostile to Paul was bound to make headway.

The Elders therefore had a practical plan to propose. Paul should participate in a ritual act in the Temple. He was to take part in a ceremony of discharging the vows of four Nazirites, who were

Below:
Jerusalem and the Dome of the Rock with, in the distance, the Mount of Olives. The Mount was the scene of an assembly called by a false prophet during the troubled times in Judaea which culminated in the destruction of Jerusalem.

Facing page:
The ruins of the harbour at Caesarea. Herod the Great, seeking to increase the prosperity of his kingdom, was determined that there should be a safe, all-weather port on the Mediterranean. On the site of the old fort of Strato's Tower he built a new city and a vast artificial harbour in twenty fathoms of water—one of the true wonders of the ancient world. Herod completed his city in twelve years and named it Caesarea in honour of Augustus.

too poor to pay the expenses of the prescribed sacrifices. Josephus tells us (*Antiquities* XIX. 294) that in such a case it was regarded as a pious act to sponsor the exercises and to join in them publicly. This involved (see *Numbers* VI.) abstention from wine, letting the hair grow, and avoiding all manner of defilement such as contact with a corpse. This 'separation' was to last seven days, at the end of which the devotees were to shave their heads, casting the hair in the fire 'which is under the sacrifice of the peace offerings'. Each of them had also to offer for sacrifice a ram, a ewe and a kid, baskets of bread, cake, oil cakes and wine. To pay the whole expenses of five such votaries involved a considerable outlay. But Paul realized what a sensible suggestion it was—this public vindication of himself as a loyal Jew, and a benevolent one at that. It would clear Paul of slander, and would clear the Elders of the charge of having welcomed an enemy of the Law and of God for the sake of money.

Paul was in fact putting into practice what he had announced in one of his letters to the *Corinthians* (1 IX. 20–22): 'And unto the Jews I became as a Jew, that I might gain the Jews; to them that are under the law, as under the law, that I might gain them that are under the law; to them that are without law, as without law, (being not without law to God, but under the law to Christ,) that I might gain them that are without law. To the weak became I as weak: I am made all things to all men, that I might by all means save some.'

The plan seemed wise and conciliatory. Unfortunately it turned out disastrously, and led directly to Paul's imprisonment and ultimately to his death. At the time of a religious feast—even to-day—Jerusalem is a tinder-box: the slightest spark, kindled wittingly or unwittingly, may ignite the fires of fanaticism. It was in such a conflagration that Paul was caught.

All went well until the seventh day, the last of the seclusion in the Temple. On that day Paul was

recognized by some Jews from Asia. At once they instigated a riot, crying out, as such rioters ordinarily do, that their holy religion had been blasphemed, that Paul had slighted the Temple, and had gone so far as to pollute it by bringing into it Trophimus, a Gentile from Ephesus. Paul had been seen walking with him in the city but he certainly had not brought him into the Temple, that is into the *sacred* portion of it, from which Gentiles were explicitly excluded by a number of notices, carved on stone in the Greek language, warning them that to transgress the injunction involved death, for which the trespasser would be responsible.

The riot spread, Paul was mobbed, and dragged out of the sacred precinct into the so-called Court of the Gentiles. The great doors of the shrine were shut. They were about to kill Paul when the sentry on duty in the fortress saw what was happening and at once reported to the commanding officer that a general riot was in progress. The officer called out the guard, and ran down into the great precinct. At the sight of the troops the mob gave way. The officer, having rescued Paul from lynching, told his men to secure him with two ropes, that is, to manacle him between two soldiers. He then demanded of the mob who their victim was and what he had done. Pandemonium broke out, everyone shouting against everyone else. The officer ordered the guard to take Paul up into the fortress. By the time they reached the great staircase which led up into the keep the mob was so violent that the soldiers were, literally, carrying him.

To understand what exactly was happening and about to happen it is necessary to understand a little of the topography of the Temple region. This can be understood from a glance at the illustration.

When Herod rebuilt the Temple, he enlarged the outer court to its greatest extent, that is thirty-five acres. Not being of priestly family he could never enter the inner courts himself, and so made the outer as sumptuous as possible. As part of this project, he extended it to the north so that it abutted the foundations of his great Antonia fortress, named after his patron Mark Antony. The illustration clearly shows the fortress on the upper right. The fortress was 370 feet long, with corner towers of which three were 75 feet high and the south-east tower 100 feet. This vast fortress contained barracks, courtyards, and a sumptuous palace for the procurator when he was on a visit to Jerusalem. It completely dominated the Temple as Herod always intended that it should. From the Antonia, one staircase led down to the roof of the cloisters and another gave direct access to the

This antique bronze portrays Berenice, the sister of King Agrippa II. A woman of great beauty, she was believed by her contemporaries to be living in incest with her brother.

Facing page:
A reconstruction of the Temple which Jesus knew and which was the scene of the tremendous events of both the New Testament and the rebellion which led to the Temple's destruction in AD 70. This Temple was the third, built by Herod the Great, who also built the Antonia fortress which can be seen above the Temple itself. The fortress stood on the north-west corner; the entrance to the Temple precinct was by way of the ramps up to the south wall and through the domed gate which led to the Court of the Gentiles—beyond which only Jews could proceed. Paul was probably dragged down the steps which led to the Court of the Women when the mob attacked him (*Acts* XXI).

Temple. There is still a staircase leading from the area up to the minaret, and to stand at the top of it is to visualize in exact detail the mortal peril in which Paul stood.

It had been a very close thing; but Paul was by this time perfectly used to riots, and to being the most hated man in the city. He now with almost unbelievable calm turned to the troop-commander and said, in Greek: 'May I speak unto thee?' 'Canst thou speak Greek?' asked the astonished officer, 'Art not thou that Egyptian, which before these days madest an uproar . . .?' Paul replied:

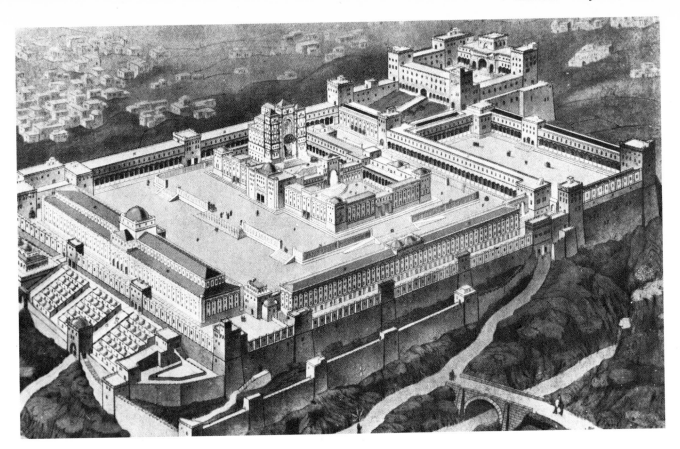

'I am a man which am a Jew of Tarsus, a city in Cilicia, a citizen of no mean city: and, I beseech thee, suffer me to speak unto the people'. (*Acts* XXI. 37–40). The officer was so taken aback that, despite the security risk involved, he agreed.

Paul had again taken command of the situation. Standing at the top of the stairs, he turned to the mob and switching from Greek to Aramaic, bade them be silent. The effect of hearing their own tongue from the lips of this 'atheist' was immediate: the multitude who had hitherto been clamouring for his death was of a sudden hushed. Paul then gave them an apologia for his life and conduct. He delivered a precise and honest resumé—birth in Tarsus, education in Jerusalem under Gamaliel, zeal in persecution, imprisonment and execution of 'heretics', journey to Damascus, conversion, return to Jerusalem, trance in the Temple, divine commission, and God's order to leave Jerusalem, despite his protest that it was he who had agreed to Stephen's death. And finally God's command that he go among the Gentiles. . . .

In a trice, at the mention of the word 'Gentiles' the riot started again, accompanied by renewed demands for Paul's death. Garments were rent, dust flung up into the air. The commanding officer, regretting his indulgence, had Paul brought into the fortress, and ordered that he be 'examined', that is flogged, so as to find out why he was the

focus of such dangerous enmity. As the warders were adjusting the thongs, Paul said to the centurion in charge: 'Is it lawful for you to scourge a man that is a Roman, and uncondemned?'

A Roman! The centurion rushed to the garrison commander, Lysias, who at once came to Paul. 'Art thou a Roman?' Paul confirmed that he was. The captain gazed wrily at his prisoner. 'With a great sum,' he said 'obtained I this freedom.' (meaning his Roman citizenship). 'I', said Paul, 'was free born.' The flogging-party was hastily dismissed, and the poor captain was left wondering how he would be able to explain the day's proceedings. Perhaps the Jewish authorities would help?

Accordingly, the next morning, the Sanhedrin was summoned and Paul cited to appear before it. The presiding officer was Ananias, son of Nebedaios, a former High Priest. He was one of those who had been sent to Claudius in the year 52 (p.oo). He returned wearing an outward virtue as white as snow, and at once proceeded to exploit his authority for his own greedy benefit. Josephus tells us (*Antiquities* XX. 206; *Wars* II. 243) that although he was no longer the reigning High Priest his prestige was such, his rapacity so barefaced, that he and his adherents were able to divert to their own use and disposal the greater portion of the meat offered as sacrifices. Not content with this, they sent their minions to the

97

Left, above:
A leaf from the fifth-century *Codex Bezae*, a Graeco-Latin manuscript of the Gospels and Acts which is of great importance in New Testament studies because it is believed to preserve the correct text of some passages which in the past have been cause for argument among scholars. The passage shown here contains the matter of *Acts* XIX, when Paul was teaching in Ephesus.

Left:
Rhodes, looking east to the town and acropolis of Lindos. The beautiful island, with its flourishing trade and centres of learning, was Paul's last contact with the Greek world.

The theatre at Ephesus, which held 24,000 spectators when filled to capacity. It was here that the famous silversmiths' riot described in *Acts* XIX took place.

very threshing-floors to carry off the tithes, which were due not to these opulent prelates but to the poor and humble members of the priesthood, many of whom, says Josephus, died of want in consequence.

Such was the man who now presided at Paul's examination. As soon as Paul began to speak Ananias ordered one of those present to strike him on the mouth. Paul answered by telling Ananias that he was a whited wall, and that God would smite him who had dared to order, contrary to the law, that an unconvicted man be struck. The court pretended to be horrified at this reviling of 'God's High Priest'. Paul, with calm irony, replied that he had not realized that it was a High Priest who had thus violated the law.

What would have been the outcome of this unsatisfactory slanging match we do not know. Paul, knowing that the Sanhedrin was composed not only of the high-priestly clique of Sadducees but also of a number of Pharisees, astutely announced that he was a Pharisee, which was true, and that if he were going to be called in question concerning the resurrection of the dead . . . At once the court dissolved in chaos and dissension. The Pharisees perforce rallied in Paul's defence, against the Sadducees, who strenuously denied the resurrection or the existence of angels and spirits: they were a hard materialist lot. Hearing the uproar (for the Sanhedrin met within the Temple precincts) Lysias sent some soldiers down to rescue Paul for the second time.

Thereupon some forty fanatics bound themselves by an oath that they would neither eat nor drink until they had murdered Paul. They suggested that the Sanhedrin should request that Paul be again brought before them, and promised that they would kill him on the way to court. But whispers of the plot reached the ears of Paul's nephew, and with all his uncle's boldness he went straight to the Antonia and warned his uncle. Paul called one of the centurions and said: 'Bring this young man unto the chief captain: for he hath a certain thing to tell him'. The centurion did as Paul bade him, explaining to the astonished officer that it was at Paul's request that he did so: so authoritative had this strange prisoner already become. The officer took the lad by the hand, and led him aside. He asked what the boy wanted to tell him. Paul's nephew explained the plot, adding that the conspirators were only waiting for Lysias' consent. After binding the boy to silence, Lysias got busy: he was taking no more risks with this Roman citizen. He called two centurions, and ordered them to assemble a detachment of 200

infantry and 70 horsemen, together with 200 auxiliaries, to be ready to leave three hours after sunset. Paul was to be provided with a relay of mounts, to get him safely to the governor, Felix, at Caesarea. The escort may seem unduly large, just to accompany one man down one of the most frequented highroads in the country; but its size is yet one more proof of how utterly insecure the whole land had become.

Lysias wrote a hurried note outlining the affair, and sent it to Felix by the hand of the officer in charge, adding that so far as he could make out Paul had committed no crime; his accusers would shortly appear before Felix. (In his outline, Lysias said that knowing Paul to be a Roman citizen, he had rescued him by force, whereas in reality he only discovered Paul's citizenship later. And he made no mention of the binding or intended flogging. These very human adjustments, like Lysias 'taking Paul's nephew by the hand', are surely hallmarks of authenticity?)

By forced marches the party reached Antipatris, the castle which Herod the Great had named after his father Antipater. It stood above the stream the Yarkon, which to-day supplies Jerusalem with part of its water-supply, supplementing that brought from Solomon's Pools in the south and the 'Valley of the Twenty-third psalm' to the north-east. It is therefore known as Ras-el-'Ain, *head of the spring*, the site being crowned by the ruins of a medieval castle. Antipatris was nearly fifty miles from Jerusalem, and almost under the aegis of Caesarea; so leaving the cavalry to escort Paul thither, the main body returned to Jerusalem.

On arrival at Caesarea, Paul was taken to Felix. After reading Lysias' letter, he asked Paul what province he came from, to which Paul answered 'Cilicia'. Felix then ordered that he be accommodated in the palace which Herod the Great had built as part of his reconstruction of the town, or rather construction, for it had been but Strato's Tower before. The work had taken twelve years.

Five days later, Ananias appeared together with the elders, and a certain advocate called Tertullus. Tertullus' speech, as recorded by Luke, has an absolutely familiar ring to anyone acquainted with the orations of modern Palestinian advocates in similar circumstances. It starts with nauseating flattery—he even thanked Felix for the prevailing 'security'—proffered with mock humility; goes

The Western or 'Wailing' Wall, all that is left of the Temple. A holy places for pious Jews for 2,000 years, the massive stone blocks of Herod's original construction were part of the southern end of the west wall.

St Paul's Bay, on the north-east of Malta, where Paul's ship was wrecked after leaving Crete. The little beach of Mistra is at the end of the inlet which lies to the left of the two great rocks at the mouth of the bay.

Facing page:
The remains of former glory. Tyre was one of the great cities of the ancient world, the pride of the Phoenicians, and already old when Rome was founded. Paul's ship called here to unload on his last journey back to Jerusalem, and here Paul heard the news that Judaea was seething with dangerous discontent.

Left:
Sidon, Tyre's sister city and with an equally proud history, is even less than Tyre in the modern world. The ruins are of a Crusader castle, while the fishing boat could belong to almost any century.

103

on to make wild accusations unsupported by evidence and but little related to the facts in question, takes care to denounce to the supreme authority the acts and motives of the subordinate on the spot (in this case Lysias) and ends with a confident appeal to justice (*Acts* XXIV. 2–8). The yes-men murmured support of this noble oration.

Paul, in his reply, after tactfully acknowledging that Felix had had long experience of legal proceedings in Judaea, said that he would very cheerfully answer for himself. He went over the familiar ground of his upbringing and faith, of his belief in a resurrection, and described his recent arrival in Jerusalem only twelve days before, bearing alms for his people. He had done nothing wrong: it was merely his insistence on the resurrection that had caused strife. Felix was impressed with Paul: he decided therefore, like a good bureaucrat, to temporize. He must wait, he said, until Lysias himself arrived. Meanwhile Paul was to be kept in custody, but his friends were to have free access to him.

A few days later Felix and his wife Drusilla decided to hear Paul again. Paul delivered one of his usual discourses; but when he came to speak of justice, and chastity, and a judgement to come, Felix began to tremble: his conscience could not stand it. He would hear Paul some other time, he said. He kept on seeing Paul, in the hope that a large bribe might be forthcoming as the price of his freedom. On the other hand in order to please Ananias and his party, he did not scruple to keep under arrest a man who was innocent in Roman law. For two years this captivity lasted, because Paul would not compromise his innocence by paying to have it admitted. By an irony of history, those two years were of incalculable value to the infant Church. They enabled Paul to establish close ties with the Christians of Palestine and Syria, and they gave Luke an opportunity to acquaint himself at first hand with the acts and the memories of the first disciples of Jesus.

Towards the middle of the year 60, Porcius Festus came to Judaea as procurator in succession to Felix, who was recalled to Rome. He was followed there by the leaders of the Caesarea Jews, who were determined to ask Caesar to punish the outgoing governor. They might well have succeeded, but for the intervention of Pallas, Felix's brother, who still had considerable influence with Nero.

Three days after reaching his capital, Caesarea, Festus went up to Jerusalem. The resentful pontiffs, having failed to secure their prey at the hands of Felix, at once approached his successor in the hope that he would prove more pliable. They even

suggested that Paul should be sent back to Jerusalem—planning to have him murdered on the way, for it must be remembered that the 'security' which Tertullus had sycophantically lauded had now ceased to exist, and that one more assassination by the *sicarii* could easily be committed without fear of detection. Festus replied that if the prelates cared to come to Caesarea he would hear them there. Ten days later he went back to his capital.

Once again, the hierarchs followed, once again they made their unproven allegations against Paul. Festus was tired of the case: was it to drag on for another two years? He tried to compromise. Would Paul agree to be judged in Jerusalem, as his accusers wanted, provided that he, Festus, presided at the trial, thus safeguarding Paul's rights as a Roman citizen, and absolved him from any sentence save that of Festus himself? Paul rejected this shabby subterfuge. He was a Roman citizen, an innocent man; why should he be sacrificed to political expediency? All he asked was justice. He

The north-west corner of the Temple area as it is today.

advantage both Agrippa's prestige as a Jewish king and his authority as one learned in Jewish law. Agrippa had the further title to be regarded and consulted, in that, although he had no territorial jurisdiction in Judaea he had the privilege of appointing the High Priests, and of having the custody of the sacred vestments. He had a residence in Jerusalem. If Paul was to go before Caesar, it was essential that Festus should state a case, in the preparation of which Agrippa would be of great help.

Festus deferentially asked Agrippa to preside at the hearing. When bidden by Agrippa, Paul 'stretched forth the hand'—his characteristic gesture —and once again gave an account of his beliefs, including that in the resurrection, and an apologia for his life and ministry. Once again, he told the story of his conversion, and his mission to the Gentiles. He kept, he said strictly to the message of the prophets and of Moses 'That Christ should suffer, and that he should be the first that should rise from the dead, and should shew light unto the people, and to the Gentiles'. At this point Festus burst out: 'Paul, thou art beside thyself: much learning doth make thee mad!' 'I am not mad' answered Paul, 'but speak forth the words of truth and soberness. For the King knoweth of these things, before whom also I speak freely: for I am persuaded that none of these things are hidden from him; for this thing was not done in a corner. King Agrippa, believest thou the prophets? I know that thou believest'.

Agrippa, in a bantering mood, said: 'Almost thou persuadest me to be a Christian'. To which Paul answered: 'I would to God, that not only thou, but also all that hear me this day, were both almost, and altogether such as I am, except these bonds'.

That ended the session. The king, the governor, with Berenice and their suite, left the court. In private discussion they agreed that Paul had done nothing deserving of death or even imprisonment. Agrippa told Festus that if Paul had not appealed to Caesar he might have been set at liberty, which was another way of assuring Festus that as Paul had appealed to Caesar, Festus was well rid of him, and could set his mind at ease (*Acts* XXVI. 32). And so Paul set out on the last stage of his life's journey, to Rome. It was the year 60.

appealed to Caesar, as he was entitled to do. Festus conferred with his council. Paul was within his rights, they said: Paul had appealed to Nero, and to Nero he must go.

A few days later, Agrippa II arrived in Caesarea having come down from his northern kingdom, the former tetrarchy of Philip son of Herod the Great athwart the source and upper reaches of the Jordan, with certain detached appanages. He was accompanied by his sister, Berenice, who now that her hated sister Drusilla was no longer there, was glad to revisit the land of her ancestors. Morally, she was no better than her sister. Twice widowed, she had deserted her third husband to live in what was all too widely reported to be incest with her brother Agrippa. (Later on she was to acquire even more notoriety as the mistress of the emperor Titus.)

Festus saw an opportunity of turning to his own

The wealthy Roman's passion for interior decoration can be seen in this remarkable mosaic from the ruins of Herculaneum, depicting the sea god Neptune and his consort Amphitrite.

Right:
A mosaic portrait of Virgil from Sousse in Tunisia which is strikingly different from the bust in the Capitoline Museum. Virgil and Horace represented the brighter side of the Roman world under the first emperors and Virgil, who is believed to have been the son of a potter and a He sits between the Epic and Tragic muses, holding a scroll of his *Aeneid*.

Facing page:
The Bay of Naples, with Vesuvius in the background. Paul's ship sailed to the north side, to Puteoli, passing on the way both Herculaneum and Pompeii. Both cities were obliterated for centuries when Vesuvius erupted in AD 79.

CHAPTER TEN

'O ROME, MY COUNTRY, CITY OF THE SOUL!'

The journey on which Paul was now about to set out was to prove among the most important ever undertaken by man. It was to be a voyage of discovery as important, as consequential in the spiritual sphere, as those of Columbus and Cook were to become in purely human evolution.

But before, with Paul and Luke, we embark on that fateful navigation, it will be well to have clearly in our minds just why Paul undertook it. His motives and his determination may easily be obscured by the actual manner of his setting out. He was after all no longer his own master; he was a prisoner, on his way to Rome under arrest. Just what he was accused of no one seemed to know but that he was a trouble-maker, in a land where quite enough trouble had been made already, was beyond question. It is also beyond question that if Paul had been willing to compromise, he need not have made the journey at all. The overriding point is that Paul was absolutely determined to reach Rome. He had formed the resolution some time before, had announced it to his disciples; he was not to be diverted from it. Just how he arrived in the world's capital was secondary, immaterial really, to a man already 'bound in spirit'.

What lay behind this irrefragable resolve? The positive side of it we will briefly examine when we reach Rome; but it is well to say something of what may be called the negative side, because it throws into sharp relief not only Paul's spiritual single-mindedness, but also what may be styled his spiritual sagacity.

That Paul and the elders in Jerusalem were by no means at one with each other has already become evident. The elders were conservative, Paul was an innovator. As he told his beloved *Philippians* (III. 13) '. . . forgetting those things which are behind, and reaching forth unto those things which

are before, I press toward the mark for the prize of the high calling in God in Christ Jesus'. This may seem simple enough to us, hackneyed almost; but to Paul's contemporaries it was novel in the extreme, because throughout antiquity, from the days of Hesiod in the eighth century BC until those of Dio in the second century AD, the 'good days', the 'golden age' was invariably thought of as being in the past. If, like Virgil, a man wanted to fortell future felicity, he did it not by forecasting novelty, but by evoking antiquity.

That basic divergence of outlook, that difference in orientation, would have made any real and abiding agreement between Paul and the Jerusalem elders impossible. But there was more to it than that. Paul, with his international experience realised that as a mother-church, a metropolitan centre, the church of Jerusalem was not viable. It would, he felt, wither. He may not have seen just how that would come about, but he was right in believing that it would.

The first step in the decline could hardly have been foreseen. In the year 62, Festus died while in office. Once again, as after Pilate's recall, this involved an interregnum, and once again it was exploited for action against the Christians. This is no coincidence. Indeed, it leads us to ask why had not the nascent church been more frequently persecuted? The answer may be found in a passage in the *Apology* of Tertullian (V. 1).

'Tiberius then in whose time the name of

Mantegna's painting of the martyrdom of James, 'the Lord's brother' of *Mark* VI. 3. The brother of Jesus, he was with Peter the leader of the infant Christian community at Jerusalem. A victim of the Sadducees' hatred, he was put to death by order of the Sanhedrin. The king, Agrippa II, failed to prevent the crime.

Right:
The Temple of Vesta in the Forum, Rome, an example of the many changes the city saw during the empire. Paul would have seen a temple to the goddess on the same spot, but it would have been an earlier, less elegant building.

Below:
The mosaic in the apse of the church of St Paul without the Walls.

Facing page, above:
Pompeii, looking from the Forum toward Caligula's arch. The Rome to which Paul journeyed was largely transformed by the later emperors. Pompeii was preserved in her original form by the eruption of Vesuvius and the remains are those of the time of Paul.

Below:
Paul's memorial church is south of the walls of Ancient Rome. Peter's is across the Tiber to the west, and today the heart of the Christian church to which both Peter and Paul gave their lives.

Christian was first heard in the world, when he received news from Palestine (which made known the truth of the divinity of Christ) brought the matter up in the Senate assigning it priority as imperial business. The Senate, because it was not itself the prime mover in the matter, rejected the motion. The emperor none the less held to his determination, and issued a warning against those who should accuse Christians.' On which Father Crehan comments: 'One can see that the phrase about "truth of the divinity of Christ" is due to Tertullian himself. What Tiberius put in his message to the Senate can only be conjectured. The Senate was in the habit of showing displeasure when it had not initiated any matter referred to it by the emperor. That the emperor should then issue an edict to damp down the affair in Palestine need not be surprising. The Tertullian passage is in Eusebius, also in Orosius and the Chronicon Paschale, which dates it to AD 35, rightly or not'.

If anti-Christian moves were thus banned, clearly an interregnum was a godsend to those who wanted to make them. It happened that at Festus' death the High Priest of the year (for Agrippa II had been compelled to yield at least this to the extremists) was Ananus, one of the five sons of the High Priest Annas of the Gospels, all of whom were to attain the supreme pontificate. A rigid Sadducee, to the accumulated pride of his family

he added a vindictive insolence of his own. As in 37, it was resolved to exploit the interval during which the local Roman authority was in abeyance. While Festus' successor was on his way, Ananus, quite illegally, arrested the elders of the Christian community, including their chief 'the brother of Jesus who was called Christ, whose name was James'. (This is not the only mention of Jesus in Josephus, but it is nevertheless a very significant one: *Antiquities* XX, IX. I.) Paul the Pharisee had escaped their snares: Ananus would be revenged on those who had harboured and encouraged him.

For twenty years, ever since the execution of James the son of Zebedee by Agrippa I, and the attempted killing of Peter, the Church had lived unmolested. During all that time James the brother of Jesus had been its head. To the Sadducees his asceticism, his strict regard for the Law, his saintly gentleness—these virtues could not compensate for the fact that he was in communion with societies who admitted converts without full compliance with the Law, that this way of life was plainly superior to theirs; and finally that he was the recipient of sums of money which they

An altar carving in the church of Sta Giustina in Padua by the sixteenth-century French artist Richard Taurin. From left to right it depicts Paul's conversion, his preaching and his arrest.

could not lay hands on—these made him the victim of their hatred.

After a trial before a packed Sanhedrin, James was hustled away to the south-east corner of the Temple, thrown down onto the unconsecrated ground below, stoned and given the *coup de grâce* by a blow from a fuller's mallet. 'The most equitable of the citizens,' says Josephus, 'were disgusted by this illegal butchery.'

That the Church was thus deprived of its head was a grievous blow; but far worse was to follow. As we have seen—and as Paul from his own experience was only too painfully aware—security was dissolving, fanaticism was inflaming the populace, and Rome, through its corrupt and insensitive servants, was hastening the inevitable catastrophe. As Tacitus puts it in a famous phrase (*History* v. 10), 'The patience of the Jews held out until the time of Gessius Florus' (last of the procurators, appointed in 64) 'then war broke out'. That was in 66.

Hostilities began with the rout of the Roman governor of Syria, Cestius Gallus, after which many prominent Jews withdrew from Jerusalem, 'as from a sinking ship'. With them went the small Christian community. They had been taught by their Master to render unto Caesar the things that are Caesar's. They could not take part in a rising against Rome. At the same time, the recent murder of James had shewn them that they could expect no clemency from Rome's adversaries. They therefore left Jerusalem, crossed the Jordan, and settled in Pella, now Tel el Fahl, in the fertile plain on the east bank of the Jordan, almost opposite Beisan. Pella was a city of the Decapolis, that is to say predominantly Greek, but it appears at this period to have formed part of Agrippa's dominions. Agrippa, besides being busy in Jerusalem where he hoped, unsuccessfully, to play the role of mediator, had no desire to incite violence against anyone. On the contrary it is to his credit that he did all in his power to halt it.

He failed, and the terrible war went inexorably on for five years, until Jerusalem lay in ruins. (The last Jewish stronghold did not fall until two years after that.)

At the head of the little Church was Symeon, nephew of James the brother of Jesus; in the first days of Christianity a sort of caliphate was almost established. So, when they returned to Jerusalem, it was Symeon who presided over the little gatherings held in a house on the site of the room of the Last Supper.

We now note the relevance of this church and its adventures to Paul and his mission. It had been

prudent, it had been submissive, it had survived. But it was less than ever the Great Church which Paul envisaged, the Church which he knew to be essential to the fulfilment of his world-wide mission. For one thing, it was feeble and enclosed, in the second place it was wholly Jewish. So much so, that when in 107, Symeon suffered martyrdom, it was not because he was a Christian but because he was a Jew that he was killed—as a descendant of David, and so a possible focus of Jewish nationalism.

It is not necessary to labour the point that Jerusalem could never be the centre of Paul's Universal Church. In fact Jewish nationalism was to revive, disastrously for Jewry, in the next century. In the disaster, the very sites of Christian devotion, the sites of the Nativity at Bethlehem and of the Sepulchre in Jerusalem were to be obliterated. Only in the fourth century were they to be rescued, and gloriously adorned by Helena, mother of the Christian emperor Constantine. But by that time Rome had long, long, been the acknowledged centre of Christendom, and its bishop the chief among his peers. Jerusalem was not even second: Byzantium, New Rome, was that. Nor did Jerusalem ever recover its primacy.

Thus has history vindicated Paul's far-sightedness. To anticipate but a few years, as early as the year 95 or 96— that is little more than a generation after Paul's death, we find the Bishop of Rome, Clement, writing a letter to the church of Corinth in which he reproves them in the matter of some dismissed presbyters, and assumes, without actually saying so, that as Bishop of Rome he is entitled to give them authoritive guidance. We cannot imagine the Bishop of Corinth writing in the same tone to the church at Rome. As has been well said, the primacy of the see of Rome was felt before it was defined. That is to say, Paul's foresight was vindicated, his great ambition achieved.

Returning now to Paul himself, we read in *Acts* XXVII. 1 that immediately after the interview with Agrippa described in the preceding chapter '. . . it was determined that we should sail into Italy'. The word 'we' shows that Luke had rejoined Paul. (The book of *Acts* contains 1,005 verses, of which 97, about a tenth of the book, are written in the first person plural.)

The actual journey to Rome, so full of episode and drama, including the most famous shipwreck in history, is given in great detail by Luke. It occupies no less than 60 verses of the book. Why this emphasis on a mere voyage? Various reasons can be suggested. Luke, being a Greek, is naturally interested in any maritime adventure. He also wants his friend Theophilus to realise what a near thing it had been for him, Theophilus: 'If Paul had been drowned', he might have thought, 'I shouldn't now be a Christian'. But above and beyond all, is Luke's conviction that this journey was the most important by far of those recorded in his book.

'And when it was determined that we should sail into Italy, they delivered Paul and certain other prisoners unto one named Julius, a centurion of Augustus' band.' This centurion is represented by Luke, in accordance with his usual practice, as being on good terms with Paul, the Roman citizen who always got on so well with Romans, the inference being—and it is vital to Luke's whole attitude—that there is nothing in the Christian message inimical to Rome. Julius is the last, and by no means the least, proponent of this basic thesis. Just what the 'Augustan band' was, we do not know. It may have been one of the five cohorts then on permanent garrison duty in Judaea; or it might have been a cohort of the Praetorian Guard, of which Julius had been in charge of a detachment forming a guard of honour for Festus, and now returning to Rome. The 'certain other prisoners' were probably lowly criminals, destined for slaughter in the theatres of Rome.

The autumn was drawing on, and soon the seas would be closed for the winter. Pliny tells us (II. 47) that the pirates (whom Pompey had eradicated) were the first to venture out in the winter, followed in his own day by misers, that is gamblers. Herod the Great had risked it in 40 BC, when it was a question of saving his throne; and as usual that remarkable man just brought it off. Josephus, who tells us the story, was not so fortunate. He made the same journey as Paul, four years later than Paul, and was wrecked. Out of a ship's company of 600 only 80 survived, including Josephus.

The Greeks had always been sea-people: the Romans on the other hand loathed the sea. Their empire was a land empire, held together by the Roman roads. Even when a sea-crossing was shorter, as for instance between Italy and Spain, they deliberately chose the détour by land. It was not surprising therefore that no ship on the direct run to Italy was available at Caesarea. The best Julius could find was a Greek ship from Adramyttium, a port of the Troad, at the bottom of the gulf of the same name east of Assos. It was an important centre and the venue for the assembly (*conventus*) of western Asia. Together with Paul and the other prisoners, there embarked Luke and Aristarchus of Thessalonika, who had been involved in the tumult at Ephesus. These two either

sailed as private passengers or more probably were carried free, as notional 'slaves' of Paul; a Roman citizen, even a prisoner, being allowed a pair to wait on him.

The day after leaving Caesarea the ship put in at Sidon, the twin city of Tyre and reputed birthplace of Dido Queen of Carthage. Paul had already gained the friendship of Julius, who allowed him to go ashore and meet his friends. The next day the ship encountered adverse winds. Instead of making a north-easterly course towards Myra, that is south of Cyprus, they had to go to the east of it so as to enjoy some protection from the westerly wind. Ancient ships were square-rigged; they could not sail into the wind nor could they tack, except to a very limited degree—even less than an Arab dhow. So it was that Paul and his companions were carried towards Cilicia, and then crept along the coast to Myra. This port was a recognized haven of refuge from the prevailing west winds. Little is left of it today; but from the ruins of its theatre, of which forty-seven tiers of seating are still visible, we may judge of its former size and opulence. It owes its present fame to the fact that Saint Nicholas, that is Santa Claus, was at one time its bishop, a fact of which the Turkish government is justifiably proud.

At Myra, the centurion had to look around for another ship because the one in which they had arrived from Caesarea was going no farther. Fortunately, as it seemed, he found the ancient equivalent of a clipper, that is a merchantman, engaged in the very lucrative corn-trade between Egypt and Italy. This traffic was vital to Rome. When after Actium in 31 BC Augustus became master of Egypt, he was careful to keep the country as his personal appanage, because he realised that anyone who gained control of Egypt could hold Rome to ransom. In fact, only a few years after Paul's voyage, Nero's general in command of the Roman army in Palestine, Vespasian, was to do exactly that, and so make himself emperor of Rome in AD 69.

The ship would be of about 300 tons burthen, with a mainmast amidships and a small foremast in the prow. It was already laden with grain, and now had to accommodate Julius and his charges. Just how many the whole company came to is not clear. Most codices give 276 as the complement,

The Jordan, looking south toward the Dead Sea. After the murder of James there was no safety for anyone who fell foul of the Sadducaic priesthood. The Christian community—and many Jews—left Jerusalem and settled in Pella on the east bank of the Jordan.

but *Bezae* has 'about 76', which considering the time of the year and the place seems more realistic.

The wind continued contrary, and it was only after 'many days' that the ship made Cnidus, on the mainland opposite Kos. In antiquity Cnidus was renowned for being the first community to exploit the nude. Praxiteles had created a superb statue of Aphrodite, the first of its kind because, except at Sparta, only males and male statues went naked. This he offered to the island of Kos. The priggish islanders, (whose tenuous textiles were notoriously revealing) refused it, whereupon the Cnidians snapped it up, and did very well out of the resulting tourist trade.

In order to find if possible an easier route, the captain bore down to the south, hoping to double Crete by sailing in the lee, that is to the south of the island. With difficulty, they made Fair Havens, near the city of Lasea. Fair Havens is a pretty little sandy bay, shaped like a horse-shoe. It was a safe anchorage, but hardly suited for a prolonged stay, and the voyagers would have to be there for about five months. That would mean that the cargo of grain must be landed and stored in weatherproof barns, while the ship would have to be beached and its mast and tackle put into storage. Fair Havens offered scant facilities for such a sojourn. Nevertheless Paul, drawing on his wide experience of seafaring, including shipwreck, urged them to remain at Fair Havens where they had already spent some time. He pointed out that the Day of Atonement (Yom Kippur, 10th Tishri, that is about the end of September or beginning of October) was already past, and that to press on would be hazardous, not only to the ship and its

Below, left:
'Render therefore unto Caesar. . . .' This element in the teaching of Jesus was one of the reasons the Christians withdrew from Jerusalem during the period of strife; they could expect no quarter from their enemies—nor could they effectively defend themselves. The emperor at this period was Nero, who was responsible for the first official persecution of Christians in the empire.

Below, right:
The interior of the Church of the Nativity in Bethlehem. The church was erected on what was believed to be the site of the birth of Jesus by the Emperor Constantine in the fourth century AD and rebuilt as we now see it by Justinian in the sixth.

Facing page:
Cargo being transhipped to a boat for further distribution. The foremast of the ship can be seen—a feature common to the trading vessels of the time. Detail from a mosaic at Ostia, the port of ancient Rome.

cargo, but to themselves as well.

The sailors knew this but reckoned that having wasted so much time at Fair Havens, they might at least venture another forty sea-miles westward, and winter at Phoenix (Port Lutro), which afforded adequate accommodation for the vessel, its cargo and complement. A conference was held, presided over by the centurion. The captain of the ship, its navigator and Paul himself were present. Since both the captain and the navigator were in favour of the plan, the centurion, who although he was in charge of the expedition was a landsman, felt bound to fall in with it. As it happened, a deceptively gentle south wind was now blowing, which seemed to favour the proposal. So off they set. And then disaster struck.

The dreaded north-easter called Euroclydon suddenly swept down upon them. It was hopeless to attempt to make headway against such a gale: they could only let the vessel drift. Soon they found themselves off the island of Gavdhos, in the lee of which they enjoyed a little respite. This enabled them to hoist the dinghy aboard—no easy matter in that sea. They then 'undergirded the ship'. This device has given rise to much argument as to how the ropes were adjusted, whether around the gun-wale (as Holzner believed) or under the keel. It is quite clear from the famous 'ship-relief' at Lindos, in the island of Rhodes, that the cables were passed under the keel, to prevent the timbers from starting. The danger now was that the ship would be carried into the Gulf of Sirte, between Tripolitania and Cyrenaica, where beyond the quicksands there lay nothing but a limitless desert. The sail was therefore lowered, and the hull left to the fury of the gale. Next day they started to lighten the ship, throwing grain overboard. On the third day, Luke tells us that he himself assisted at the jettisoning of the ship's tackle (*Acts* XXVII. 19).

For some days the ship simply drifted. No one knew where they were, because the sun was hidden by day and the stars by night. Gradually they gave up all hope of survival; they had not even the strength to eat. Finally Paul, as so often before, took charge. He could not forbear to say 'Sirs, ye should have harkened unto me' to the captain and sailors; but went on to announce that everybody would come through safe and sound: an angel of God had given him this assurance. Only the ship would be lost: the ship's company would be cast upon an island.

In the middle of the fourteenth night after leav-

ing Crete, the crew thought that they were nearing land: above the howling of the tempest, they could hear the booming of surf on rock. They at once took soundings. Sure enough, the line shewed only twenty fathoms, about 120 feet. A little farther on, the depth had fallen to fifteen fathoms: clearly land was near. But to be cast on those rocks meant certain death. The crew therefore dropped four anchors out from the stern, and longed for the dawn. Some of the sailors now decided that they would at least make certain of their own safety. Pretending that they were going to rig anchors from the prow, which could only be done by means of the dinghy, they started to lower it. Paul, who knew what they were up to, at once told Julius and the soldiers, 'Except these' (the deserting seamen) 'abide in the ship, ye cannot be saved'. The soldiers at once cut the dinghy's painter and let it fall off.

Paul was now in his element. When dawn approached he took matters in hand. If, as he foresaw, the ship was going to break up, it would mean swimming for the passengers and crew. They would need all the strength they could command. So Paul told them to eat something. He set the example himself, breaking a loaf in view of them all, and giving thanks to God for it. That cheered them up, and they started to eat too. When they'd had enough, they threw overboard what remained of the wheat.

It was now light. The captain did not recognize the land, nor did anyone else; but by good fortune they found themselves at the entry of a bay with a strand at the end of it, not those cruel rocks. It would be just the place to beach the ship if they could get her there. So, weighing the anchors and hoisting the mainsail, they lowered the two rudder-sweeps into the water and made for the shore. But the gale was still blowing from the east now, so that the ship, instead of making for the beach, was carried to leeward, towards a tongue of land between two arms of the sea. There it stuck fast, and started to break up. The soldiers wanted to kill the prisoners, to prevent their escaping; but Julius, determined to save Paul, ordered those who could swim to throw themselves into the sea and make for the beach—it was quite close—while the rest were to support themselves on boards and broken pieces of ship's timber. In this manner they all got safely ashore.

So ended the most famous shipwreck in history. 'And when they were escaped, then they knew that the island was called Melita.' Melita, of course, is the island we know as Malta. As to where the shipwreck occurred, there is no reason to doubt the traditional site—Saint Paul's Bay, as it is called. The soundings fit the approaches to it, and on the northern side of it—and nowhere else in Malta—there is a tongue of land between two arms of the sea. Just south of it, too, are long stretches of barren, craggy rock, over which the waves continually break in stormy weather. Within the bay, on its northern shore, is a beach called Mistra, below the old castle of Selmun. It may well have been on this very strand that Paul and the others landed. The name means in Maltese 'place of refuge' and is related to the Arabic root str meaning 'preserve'.

It is possible, on a superficial reading of Luke's narrative of the apostle's sojourn in Malta, to form the impression that the islanders were uncouth peasants. In fact they were nothing of the sort: they were prosperous artificers and artists, particularly in the production of rich textiles. They traded far and wide, making the most of their excellent harbours. It happens that we possess two witnesses to their high standard of living; the first Roman, the second Greek. Cicero, when prosecuting Verres, the corrupt and rapacious governor of Sicily (a province in which Cicero himself had served) in 70 BC, accused him of not merely plundering Sicily but of stretching out his greedy hand to ravage Malta. One Maltese had been persecuted because he possessed a fine collection of silver plate. The temple of Juno, regarded as sacrosanct even by hostile kings, had been robbed of its ivory and precious metals. Honey had been requisitioned by the hogshead; even roses had been sent for, to stuff Verres' pillows, made of delicate Malta lawn.

Writing a little later, Diodorus of Sicily has much the same tale to tell. Malta, he says, is a Phoenician, that is Carthaginian, colony of great renown. Like Cicero he praises its harbours. (In Cicero's day they had been the winter asylum of pirates, because he was speaking three years before Pompey swept them from the seas. The fact that they could find refuge for five whole months out of the twelve only seventy miles from a Roman province shews once again how rare winter navigation was.) Again we hear of the excellence of Maltese textiles, specially their linen. Weaving had always been a Phoenician speciality, and Virgil (*Aeneid* XI. 75) makes Dido herself a skilled weaver of purple and gold fabric. The inhabitants lived in beautifully situated houses, adorned with cornices and stucco walls: like Romans in fact. The magnificent temples of the neolithic age, among the finest in the world, were of course now deserted and unregarded except with a certain vague awe as

The little harbour of St Paul's Bay. In the centre is the church dedicated to Paul at the end of the sixteenth century.

the dwellings of the 'giants' of old. In such a commercial community so like his native Tarsus, Paul would soon feel at home.

News of the shipwreck soon spread. The people of Malta, then as now, were a gentle and compassionate folk, and they set to work at once to do what they could for the castaways. The first thing was to kindle a fire, to warm the shivering strangers, and everyone joined the search for fuel, scarce after such a tempest and on so rocky a terrain, even though as fortune would have it the ship had gone aground and broken up near the estate of Publius, the chief man, *prōtos* of the island. Again Luke uses accurately the technical term for the principal local representative of the Roman power, since the island was a dependency of the province of Sicily. The title is known from two inscriptions, one Greek one Latin, found in Malta.

As Paul threw his bundle of sticks (probably vine-prunings at that time of year: cf *John* xv. 6) onto the fire, a viper slid out and fastened on his hand. The late Mgr Knox suggests, in a footnote to his translation of the New Testament, that as there are no poisonous snakes in Malta, it may have found its way to the island in one of the African grain ships. The bystanders were startled. 'No doubt this man is a murderer,' they said, 'whom, though he hath escaped the sea, yet vengeance suffereth not to live.' Paul merely shook the creature off and went on with his wood gathering, unharmed. Then the populace noticed something; the officer in charge of the troops on board treated this man with deference. Then someone discovered that the stranger could speak a language the peasants could understand. The Maltese spoke a Punic, that is a Semitic tongue, and the stranger, though evidently he knew Latin and Greek from the way he conversed with the ship's company, also talked Aramaic, which was quite easy for them to get along in. With the quicksilver emotion of a crowd

119

the people hailed as a god the man they had but lately called a murderer.

It was now clear that the whole company would have to winter in Malta, that it would be at least three months before they could continue their journey. Paul and Luke had no desire to be a burden on their kind hosts: Paul was always a stickler for that. After being the guests of Publius for three days, they moved into quarters of their own, and at once set about doing what they could for the islanders. Luke's medical skill, seconded by Paul's charismatic gift of therapy, soon found scope. Their first patient was Publius' father, who was suffering from dysentery. He was cured. Other sufferers soon flocked to the heaven-sent healers. By the time they were to leave the island, three months later, they were so highly regarded that they lacked for nothing—the generous and grateful Maltese saw to it that they were fully equipped, and the loss of all their luggage made good. Publius himself joined the new Way, and is now venerated as the first Bishop of Malta.

It happened that an Alexandrian corn-ship had been wintering in Malta in the great harbour at the southern end of the island now known as Marsaxlokk. This affords—as the Valetta harbours do not—snug anchorage against the eastern gales. The ship was called the *Castor and Pollux*, the protectors of sailors. It was still only February, but the captain reckoned that for such a short journey it was worth taking a bit of a risk, because the reward of being among the first 'clippers' of the season would be great. They crossed to Syracuse without incident, and stayed there for three days. Today this storied city, which had seen the downfall of Athenian pride and the death of Archimedes, bears abundant witness in its catacombs and early churches to the faith of which Paul was the harbinger. Its most eloquent testimony is unique—the cathedral. This was formerly a temple of Athena, and is now the only Doric temple to be still used as a place of worship.

The next port of call was Rhegium (Reggio), on the Italian side of the straits of Messina, beyond

the perils of Scylla and Charibdis. Now, safely in Italian waters, they could hug that beautiful and historic coast. Up they sailed past the palace of Tiberius on Capri, past the villas of the rich which jutted out into that smiling bay, past Pompeii and Herculaneum and the unsuspected Vesuvius which nineteen years later was to obliterate them, and so to Puteoli (Pozzuoli), the port of Rome for travellers from the east.

Much of Roman Puteoli is now, owing to seismic displacement, under the water; but enough remains, including a great brick amphitheatre (later than Paul's day), to suggest to us what a thriving, busy, bawdy harbour it must have been. Yet even here, in this unlikely, undivine milieu, there was a company of Christians. Even more surprising is the fact that Julius, who must have been longing for Rome, allowed his charge to spend a whole week there. No doubt the arrival of the ship had caused quite a sensation. Seneca tells us (*Letters to Lucilius* LXXVII. I) how the population of the town rushed down to the quays when an Egyptian grain

Above:
An engraving by the sixteenth-century Dutch artist Hendrik Goltzius shows the shipwreck (in the artist's terms of reference, not those of Paul's day) and the incident of the snake in the bundle of kindling.

Facing page:
Mistra, looking down on the beach where Paul and his companions reached land safely after the shipwreck.

Above:
Pozzuoli, in the Bay of Naples, was Puteoli in Paul's day and it was there he landed on the last stage of his journey. Apart from the amphitheatre little is left of the Roman town, most of which is now submerged in the bay.

Facing page:
The Via Appia, the road Paul trod on his way to Rome.

ship was sighted. Only these vessels were allowed to enter port dressed overall.

The rest of the journey to Rome was made on foot. In those days this involved going by way of Naples, because only in the reign of Domitian was a short cut constructed of which the vestiges still command our admiration of Roman engineering skill. The transit would take about a week for the 130 miles. They went by Formia, past the country house and cenotaph of Cicero. After leaving Terracina, they came to the Pontine marshes, across which Augustus had dug a canal alongside the road as far as the Forum of Appius. Julius and Paul may well have used it, being hauled in a barge drawn by donkeys. Horace, in one of his satires, has described a trip on it. He didn't think much of the inn at the Forum. The country was riddled with malaria: its cause was unknown, but a shrine dedicated to Aesculapius proclaimed its prevalence. Some of the Roman brethren had come as far as this to greet Paul. Others were waiting for him at the Three Taverns, thirty-three miles from the capital. Finally, travelling along the Via Appia, the very Queen of Roads, as the Romans called it, the party mounted the Alban hills. There below them lay Rome. Paul '... thanked God and took courage'.

THE ETERNAL CITY

Rome! The Eternal City, as the proud Romans were beginning to call it. It was the earthly goal of Paul's life: he had long been determined to go there, because he saw that Rome and only Rome could be the heart and centre for a viable Church.

'And when we came to Rome, the centurion delivered the prisoners to the captain of the guard: but Paul was suffered to dwell by himself with a soldier that kept him.' (*Acts* XXVIII. 16). The captain of the guard, or *stratopedarch*, implies a camp commandant, a subordinate, that is of the Praetorian Prefect. At the time of Paul's arrival, the Prefect was Burrus, a friend of Seneca, and like him a Stoic who had been a tutor to the young Nero, whose worst instincts they had been able so far to keep in check. There were nine or ten Praetorian cohorts, of 1,000 men each.

What sort of city was it to which Paul had come? What did it look like, what were its amenities? No boast was ever more misleading than that of Augustus, who is reported to have said that he found Rome brick, and left it marble. True, the famous Carrara (Luna) quarries had just been opened; but although marble might be used as we shall see in certain contexts the city itself was still largely built of brick, though with this important reservation: whereas until the time of Augustus sun-dried brick was the usual building material, kiln-baked bricks were now being manufactured. These were often faced with stucco or marble. Moreover, concrete was coming more and more into vogue.

The combination of concrete and brick was to revolutionize Roman building methods, and make possible the construction of daring vaults, one of which, the dome of the Pantheon, is still the widest in the world—thirty inches wider than that of St Peter's. But all that lay in the future. So did

most of the monuments that we today think of as being specially Roman, the hallmark of empire. The three triumphal arches, of Titus, Septimius Severus and Constantine, the Colosseum, the columns of Trajan and Marcus Aurelius, the temples of Hadrian and Antoninus, Hadrian's mausoleum, famous now as the Castel St Angelo—not one of these familiar memorials had yet been raised, and they by no means exhaust the list. On the Palatine, Tiberius had added to Augustus' simple dwelling—the remnants of his palace lie buried beneath the Farnese gardens—but the grandeur of the visible ruins is wholly the work of later ages. On the Capitol, on the other hand, the Tabularium or record office, of which we still admire the column-flanked arches, soon to become a canon of Roman official construction, goes back to 78 BC. It was to be the model for all the triumphal arches, and also for the beautiful masonry of the Theatre of Marcellus, which Augustus had erected in memory of his nephew.

Down in the Forum, there were the two basilicas, the Aemilian and the Julian, used as law courts and places of assembly. Paul could not have known that the basilica was to become the prototype of the Christian church, with the bishop presiding in the apse, as the secular judge had formerly done. In the Forum, too, he would behold the temple of Castor and Pollux, whose names his last ship had borne; the temple of Vesta (though not as we now see it), the altar of Julius Caesar, deified, the house of the Pontifex Maximus, and a medley of shops

The Porta San Paolo in Rome is the ancient Porta Ostiensis, which led the way out of the city to the harbour at Ostia. Through this gate, it is believed, Paul would have passed to his death about three miles from Rome.

and shrines. Julius' own forum lay just to the north-east.

By the river there were the two little temples we see to-day, one round one oblong, near the mouth of the great drain, the Cloaca Maxima; and not far from the temple and theatre of Pompey the four republican temples in what is now the Largo Argentina. We can still admire the vestiges of the first stone bridge Rome ever knew, the Ponte Rotto, or broken bridge erected in 179 BC by the same Aemilius as built the basilica. Two other bridges were standing in Paul's day—the Milvian bridge which carried the Via Flaminia, the Great North Road, over the Tiber, the bridge which

was to see the triumph of Constantine and Christianity in AD 312. It had been built, or re-fashioned by Marcus Aemilius Scaurus, in 109 BC. The four middle arches are still there, with their bold and unprecedented span of sixty feet. The other bridge is the Ponto Fabricio. It was built in 62 BC and is still almost intact, down to its donor's name.

Of Augustus, the founder and architect of this new 'marble age' there were three visible and personal memorials, his grand temple dedicated to Mars Ultor, 'The Avenger' that is of Julius Caesar, at the foot of the Esquiline of which a few columns still stand, together with a massive fire-proof back

wall; his grand mausoleum down by the river, and his Altar of Peace, of which more will shortly be said. Above all, there glistened on the summit of the Capitol the temple of Jupiter Capitolinus, the shrine in which were worshipped Rome's great triad, Jupiter, Juno and Minerva, destined within three centuries to yield pre-eminence to a more closely-knit Trinity. Only traces of its foundation now exist.

Such—in very brief outline, for how can the glories of Rome be shrunk into a niggardly catalogue?—were the external trappings of Roman greatness, as seen by Paul on his arrival. Of their general impact, two things may be postulated. The

Above, left:
The Forum, a view from the Capitol looking down to the arch of Titus. The arch in the foreground is that of Septimius Severus and in the middle distance to the right are the three columns of the temple of Castor and Pollux. On the far right of that are the lower slopes of the Palatine.

Above:
The ruins of the Ponte Rotto the first stone bridge of Rome. It was constructed in 179 BC and was a frequently used crossing of the Tiber in Paul's day.

127

first is that in Paul's day Rome had not yet achieved the apogee of imperial splendour that was to be hers in the next century—an important point, because the idea that Rome was already 'for the dark' is utterly misleading, especially when dealing with matters of belief and practice and their exponents. The other is that although it had not yet achieved its ultimate spacious grandeur the Rome of Augustus, of Tiberius, of Claudius and even Nero (before he reconstructed Rome after the fire of 64) was far more impressive than any city Paul had yet seen. Impressive by its complexity, its multiplicity, its aliveness.

The Romans always felt a little inferior to the Greeks, when it came to anything but fighting. They could not pretend that any single building of theirs could rival in artistic merit the finest Greek work of Athens or Delphi. But by sheer weight of numbers they could rival Greece, and did. And to crown all, Augustus had the brilliant idea of importing into his capital monuments far, far older than anything Hellas could boast, namely obelisks from Egypt.

Augustus imported two. He placed one, which dates from the time of Seti I (19th dynasty) and his son Rameses II (1348–1282 BC), in the Circus Maximus. It now stands in the Piazza del Popolo. The second of Augustus' obelisks has since 1789 stood on Monte Citorio. It was made for Psammetichus II of the 26th Dynasty. It became the gnomon of a gigantic sundial in the Campus Martius. Caligula added a third obelisk, an imitation, because it bears no hieroglyphics. It now stands in front of St Peter's. Later emperors were to add ten more of these memorials. Their importance is by no means merely decorative. Paul's contemporary Pliny tells us of the three that adorned Rome in his day. He says quite correctly that the Egyptian word for obelisk, *tekhen*, also means sunbeam, so that the obelisk is a representation of the sun god. Thus, as the inscriptions on the bases of Augustus' two obelisks inform us, they were the emperor's 'gifts to the sun'. This is of prime importance, because in the third century AD the sun-cult was to become the state religion, and being monotheistic was to help powerfully in the transition to Christianity. But that evolution would have been hidden from the eyes of Paul.

In fact, these intimations of material immortality would have meant very little to Paul. True, he tells his *Philippians* (IV. 22) that 'All the saints salute you, chiefly they that are of Caesar's household', where, as he has already assured them (I. 13) he is well known. But being Paul, he would be more immediately concerned with the humbler citizens.

The three surviving columns and rear wall of the temple built by Augustus at the foot of the Esquiline to honour Mars Ultor. Mars in this aspect was the Avenger: Augustus won the struggle for power following the murder of Julius Caesar, the 'avenged' in this particular case.

Facing page:
The Piazza del Popolo and, in the distance, St Peter's on the other side of the Tiber. The obelisk was brought to Rome by Augustus and was originally placed in the Circus Maximus. It is over 3,000 years old–cut and decorated in nineteenth-dynasty Egypt.

The Rome of his day was a plutocracy, and as in any plutocratic society, London of the last century or New York of this, alongside a small and very opulent class, highly intelligent and cultivated though it may be, there co-exists a great mass of people who live in conditions not far removed from squalor. Such certainly was the Rome of Paul's day. The poorer citizens were herded into tall blocks of flats, insanitary, ill-heated in winter, appallingly stuffy in summer. The poet Martial tells us of a man who had to climb two hundred steps to reach his room. The fire-risk was endemic. Despite the ample supplies of water which Rome's aqueducts delivered to the city, the distribution system was primitive. A few rich men could afford to have the water piped to their houses, but the majority had to be content with standpipes.

For with all their engineering skill, the Romans never developed the atmospheric pump, nor did they know how to cast iron. This meant that water could only be supplied by gravity, and through pipes made of lead, which being soft and malleable, were constantly bursting. Sanitation was exiguous. Cesspools and dungheaps lay at convenient, or inconvenient, intervals, and to these human refuse had to be carried by hand, or simply flung into the street below. Public latrines there were, often on a grand scale, fifty or more seats to a unit, provided with running water. And of course the famous baths were open to one and all.

The din was appalling (it still is in Rome). Even rich Seneca found it hard to bear. By night the heavy waggons rumbled and creaked over the rough streets. By day all sorts of wandering priests of Isis or Cybele or other exotic deities went about clanging their brass cymbals, their systra and their castanets. And everywhere were the idle crowds, waiting for a dole from some rich patron, or from the state. Many of the multitude came from overseas, from the Levant in particular; many were dispossessed peasants, whose lands had been enclosed by rich capitalists, or expropriated to find homes for veterans. Political life was dead. Only in the theatre or the circus could men assemble.

The crucial question, for the purpose of this little essay, is to what extent was Roman society really corrupt? Was it politically barren, culturally and spiritually sterile? The answer to this question has varied far more with fashion than with fact.

During the nineteenth century republics were very much in vogue. There were empires, but the only good empire, in the eyes of the beholder, was one's own, which was a special case, benign and enlightened. That was the view held by political prigs of the Victorian era. Nowadays, we cannot view things so simply. A number of empires have disappeared; but it is at least an open question whether those who formerly lived in them are in all cases better off, happier, more secure and more prosperous than in days gone by.

In the Roman empire both views were held. Some old republicans still cherished the idea that the rule of one man and his court was tyranny, and un-Roman slavery. On the other hand, a great many did not. They lauded what Pliny called '. . . the infinite majesty of the Roman peace'. After the century of intrigue and slaughter which had preceded Augustus' victory at Actium, simply to be secure, and at peace—that was the *summum bonum*. It seemed to be the gift of 'some god' sang Virgil, and Virgil was a noble Roman if ever there was one.

The poet Virgil, a bust in the Capitoline Museum.

Facing page:
The art of mosaic reached a high level in ancient Rome, and much information about life in the time of Paul can be gleaned from them. An example of the Roman artists' skill in this form can be seen in this mosaic from the temple of Fortuna at Palestrina, showing life in Egypt, from Alexandria to the confines of Ethiopia.

The story of Paul's journeys is a proof of the public tranquility that the age enjoyed. Paul did get into scrapes with the local authorities, at Lystra, at Philippi, Thessalonika and Ephesus, in Jerusalem itself; but he was always able to move on, or be moved on, because the roads were open, the seaways free of pirates. Indeed his adventures in nearly all these predicaments go to show by their issue how firmly Rome did in fact rule. When a breach of the peace occurred, order was at once restored. This firm Roman hand held the world in fee; from the Tigris to the Tweed, from Aswan to Paris, a man might travel or trade. There was in being a regional unity such as the world had never before known, nor would know again until the consolidation of the United States of America. Of this unity, this outspread security, there was no greater beneficiary than the infant Church, as the record of Paul's travels has already shewn.

The Christian view that Rome was a providential institution is established not merely by inference but by positive evidence. Tertullian, writing about AD 200, and a Persian Christian about half a century later, both had a definite idea that Rome must last as long as the world. Later still Prudentius, the great Latin Christian poet, in or about AD 380, constantly proclaimed the divine ordering of this unification of mankind: 'Christ willed the course of kingdoms in due sequence, and the triumphs of Rome, in order that, when the ages were fulfilled he might impart himself; God would bind together nations discordant in speech, various in worship, and bring all under one sway, a union of hearts; no union would be worthy of Christ, did not one mind link race ro race. Christ is author of the walls of Rome, who set the sceptre at Rome as head of the world and bade mankind submit to the Roman toga and arms, that all the jangling races might learn customs and culture, that all their tongues, their genius and their rites might know one set of laws; this was achieved by the Roman empire's successes and triumphs: the way was prepared for Christ's coming'.

Has any modern internationalist painted a more glowing picture? (The summary is Glover's.) Josephus the Jew, Epictetus the slave-Stoic, Christian apologist, and Christian poet all tell the same story. The conviction is echoed by Claudian in the very last century of the Western empire.

Bad emperors there might be, and none was worse than Nero, in whose reign Paul was executed, and by whom after the great fire of AD 64 the Christians were first persecuted as such with every refinement of revolting cruelty. Here again, we must be cautious not to condemn too widely. That not only Nero but his court as well were lewd and corrupt is beyond question. But we depend for our knowledge of it on a raffish raconteur, Suetonius (whom the emperor Hadrian found intolerable), Juvenal, a sour-minded satirist, and Tacitus, who took a gloomy view of mankind in general. Even Tacitus has to admit that despite the goings-on of the mighty, there still were decent men and women in Italy leading decent family lives. Dio, who wrote his history more than a century later, can only reflect the earlier annalists.

That there was from first to last a coarse and cruel strain in the Roman character cannot be gainsaid. But if we examine their moral and cultural standards, as we may now briefly do, we may well find that the general tone was not only more elevated than might appear at first sight, but that there was a general desire for amelioration, which

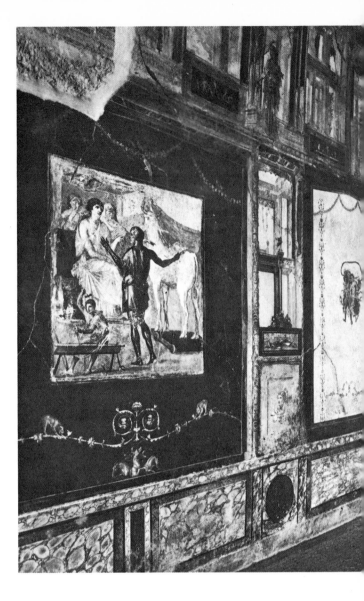

A room in a villa in Pompeii. This is one of the best preserved examples of Roman wall painting.

would discover in the message of Paul and his disciples a 'medicine for the soul' such as they had failed so far to find. This point—that in the early days of Christianity there were eager receivers as well as ardent givers—is of cardinal importance in estimating the moral climate of first-century Rome. It is true that the butchery of the amphitheatre went on until the end, that the largest of all such buildings, the Flavian amphitheatre or Colosseum was built towards the end of the century, with a capacity of 50,000; but it is also true that a high-minded Stoic such as Marcus Aurelius was ill at ease in it. He used to take state papers with him to read, rather than concentrate on the carnage. He also, having seen a rope-walker crash to death, commanded that all such acts must in future be performed over a net. And we find in the rescripts

ing for humanity. The personality of the individual is more and more a paramount theme—the personality of the individual and his relationship to his environment. Roman poetry is instinct with this feeling. Catullus, Propertius, Tibullus—as we read them, we are filled with sympathy for the sufferings of their hearts: we really do 'feel with' them. Even Ovid, raffish and louche though he all too often is, awakes in us a spark of pity for his woes. When we come to the two greatest poets of the age, both intimate friends of Augustus, we are face to face with personalities so vivid, that we are conscious of knowing them as they knew each other. Virgil was born near Mantua in 70 BC, Horace in Apulia five years later. He met Virgil in early manhood, and became devoted to him until his death in 19 BC. Horace lived until 8 BC. 'Whenever we think of "that hard Roman world"' writes Glover 'which Tacitus drew so cleverly and Juvenal lashed with epigrams, we have to remember that it was the world of Virgil, and that it loved Virgil. There is much in the famous saying of Sainte-Beuve: "la venue même du Christ n'a rien qui étonne quand on a lu Virgile"'.

Yes, Rome did love Virgil; and not only just an intellectual côterie. He became a school textbook in his own lifetime. Soldiers in remote lands scrawled lines from the *Aeneid* on the walls of their barracks.

For sheer elevation of spirit, possessed and communicated, it would be hard to find Virgil's equal. The majestic mythmaking of the *Aeneid*, the tapestry into which is woven Rome's many-hued destiny; the phrases, single words sometimes that evoke what Jackson Knight has aptly called 'the vision of the collective unconscious'—this is mixed with an intense empathy for the countryside, for fields and flocks and flowers.

To cite another French writer: 'It is impossible', says Pierre Boyance in *La Réligion de Virgile* (1963), 'at one and the same time to admire Virgil and to condemn Rome. For posterity he is Rome's most fervent but also most faithful interpreter . . . It is above all the Fourth Eclogue, it is above all the sixth book of the *Aeneid,* which was bound to give Virgil in the eyes of posterity something of the inspired prophet. It was those verses which Christianity was bound to hold to, because in them it found something of its own revelation. In them Virgil gives us the impression of rising above his times and country. He alone knew how to weld the history of Rome into that of the whole of humanity, in which the cosmos itself took a part. In that is expressed the very depth of his soul, and there souls are not deceived: he had the honour of

of his immediate predecessors such phrases as 'such conduct is not worthy of our times', clearly shewing that these emperors considered that they were living in an age not worse but better than those gone by.

If they believed this the upward trend must have started in the first century. To quote one concrete example. It was the horrible custom of the Romans, sanctioned by law, that when a citizen was killed by a slave, all that man's slaves must be put to death. Tacitus tells us (*Annals* XIV. 42) that Pedanius Secundus, when Prefect of the City, was murdered by a slave who was jealous of his master's affection for a slave girl. No less than four hundred slaves were therefore doomed. The citizens protested against this slaughter, but the emperor and senate decided to let the law takes its savage course. But the popular protest was not without effect, because we do find that by the days of Hadrian the barbarous law had been drastically modified.

If we now turn to the arts we find the same feel-

guiding Dante to the threshold of Paradise.'

Horace never aspired to the spiritual peaks. He is a very human poet, warm and witty. He can write with a grace that has never been excelled: he sang with what Petronius was to call 'painstaking happiness'. Like all the poets so far mentioned Horace combines the gift for portraying individuals, emperors, innkeepers, bores, with an intense love of the countryside, its trees, and farms and rivers, its birds and flowers. The picture of the Romans as a herd of self-indulgent townees is completely distorted.

The Romans in fact loved the country. One has only to note how perfectly they sited their villas to understand that. Not only sited them but wrote enthusiastic letters and poems about them. This trait was as strong in the last days of the empire as in the first, as we can easily gather from the pages of Ausonius, Claudian and Sidonius Apollinaris. Four other arts help in revealing to us the Roman claim to aesthetic, and thence to spiritual sensibility: mosaic, painting, stucco and sculpture.

Roman mosaics tells us in great detail just what men, women and things looked like then; gladiators—and their victims, for as already noted there was in the Roman throughout his epoch, combined with his immortal longings some extremely mortal weaknesses—hunters, charioteers, fishermen, farms and country houses. Birds and sylvan scenes are just as common as mythological pictures. These lively decorations must have given a vivid grace to the rooms they adorned.

Gradually, mosaics (still of course the stone-tessera variety, for glass mosaic, a completely different art, did not come into vogue until the Byzantine era), were applied to walls, as in the charming niches to be seen in Herculaneum and Pompeii, or the now famous representation of Christ as the Unconquered Sun in the Vatican grottos. Two of the most interesting mosaics which have survived are the one at Palestrina which shews in great detail what life was like in Egypt during the imperial epoch, and the celebrated portrait of Virgil from Sousse in Tunisia. In the fourth century we find mosaic used for decorating ceilings, as in the church of St Pudenziana in

Rome. Significantly enough, the theme in this sacred context is simply a charmingly natural country scene, with *putti* conducting a merry grape-harvest and vintage.

When we consider Roman painting, we find again that mixture of mythology and country life which Roman mosaics display. There are fine examples at Pompeii, Herculaneum, finer ones still at Stabia (Castelammare) which like them was obliterated in the eruption of AD 79. Particularly at Stabia we are looking at pictures which seem to us strikingly modern in their use of perspective, and other devices which we associate with Botticelli or the Impressionists. In Rome itself, there are two superb compositions.

The first is a red-laquered room from the Farnesina, now in the National Museum. In a magnificent *trompe l'oeil* architectural framework are hung medallions showing domestic and allegorical scenes, typical of the Roman delight in the actual and individual: even mythology must be tamed so as to become part of everyday life. But by far the most beautiful and moving example of Roman painting to survive for our delight is the painted room from the villa of Livia, Augustus' empress, at Prima Porta, a short distance north of Rome. This, too, is now in the National Museum. It is a masterpiece of Roman naturalistic art. It has an open air subject. We are in a garden, and whever we look we see nothing but the blue sky through green trees, maples, laurels, bay and cypress. In the foreground is a balustrade which marks the confines of the garden in which we stand. Beyond, fruit-trees and flowers meet our gaze on all sides. Birds are there too, and butterflies, in fact all the beauty of a summer landscape. It seems indeed, this painted garden, to breathe the spirit of peace, security and rural grace Augustus hoped with good reason that his régime had restored: it seems indeed a Golden Age into which we have stepped.

Roman stucco decoration depicts similar scenes of domestic and rural peace or spiritual liberation, as shown in the decoration of the underground basilica near Santa Maria Maggiore, the finest of all Roman stuccoed vaults. It was apparently the meeting-place of a mystical sect, perhaps Neo-Pythagorean. But the greatest single example of the Augustan ideal is to be found in a monument designed, or at least ordained, by Augustus himself. This is his *Ara Pacis,* or Altar of Peace, which originally stood on the western side of the Via Lata, the broad way, now the Corso, which brought the Via Flaminia into the heart of the city. The altar has now by a miracle of restoration been reassembled in a glazed building on the bank of the

Facing page, above:
A detail from the east side of the *Ara Pacis*. Mother Earth, and her bounty to mankind.

Below:
On the west side of the *Ara Pacis* Aeneas, safely arrived in the promised land (Italy), prepares to sacrifice a white sow to the goddess Juno in thanksgiving.

Tiber hard by Augustus' own mausoleum. It was consecrated in 13 BC.

In the words of Professor Jocelyn Toynbee (who has generously allowed their citation): 'The *Ara Pacis* expresses a more intimate sense of history, a deeper devotion to fact and actuality, in presenting contemporary, living people, some of them individuals whose identity we can fix with certainty, or with a very high degree of probability, just as they were at a given moment, on the 4th July, 13 BC. The south side is occupied by the emperor himself, with his immediate entourage of officials, priests and relations, the north side by members of the Roman religious fraternities, magistrates, senators, and other persons, with their families who walked behind. On the east facing the great highway are two groups of personifications symbolizing to all passers-by the far-reaching and enduring effects of the *Pax Romana* now solemnly established by Augustus' return [from an extensive tour of the western provinces: see Horace, *Odes*, IV. 27]—the warrior goddess Roma, seated at peace, and Tellus, or more probably the motherland of Italy, rich in children and in all the other gifts which peace bestows. On the west are two legendary scenes—Aeneas, Augustus' prototype, making the sacrifice, that offered to Juno, of the famous white sow of the prodigy, the augury for the foundation of Lavinium (Virgil, *Aeneid* VIII. 80 ff.), a sacrifice of thanksgiving for his homecoming to the promised land of Italy; and the scene of the Lupercal, where in the presence of Mars and Faustulus the she-wolf suckled Romulus and his brother.... The great acanthus dado, interwoven with vine and ivy and sheltering a lively populace of miniature birds, insects, snakes, frogs and lizards may possibly represent the freezing into marble of a ceremonial carpet laid outside the temporary enclosure over which the procession passed....

'The *Ara Pacis* has a peculiar quality.... It appeals to us by its serene tranquility, its unpretentious stateliness, its homely intimacy, its gracious informality, its delight in nature, its purposeful unity, and not least by its modest dimensions. It embodies the very best that Rome bestowed on Italy and it strikes the perfect balance between land and city on which Augustus claimed to build his empire.'

Augustus left a magnificent patrimony to those who were to come after him. An English poet has given a magnificent description of it. John Milton was in Rome in 1638 and again in 1639, during his thirty-first year. In 1671, old and blind, he published *Paradise Regained*. In the beginning of the Fourth Book, Milton places the Temptation of Jesus in Rome, which Satan describes as follows in the most majestic panorama of Roman glory ever painted:

The City which thou seest no other deem
Then great and glorious *Rome*, Queen of the
    Earth
So far renown'd and with the spoils enricht
of Nations; there the Capitol thou seest
Above the rest lifting his stately head
On the *Tarpeian* rock, her Cittadel
Impregnable, and there Mount *Palatine*
The Imperial Palace, compass high, and high
The Structure, skill of noblest Architects,
With gilded battlements, conspicuous far,
Turrets and Terrases, and glittering Spires.
Many a fair Edifice besides, more like
Houses of Gods (so well I have dispos'd
My Aerie Microscope) thou may'st behold
Outside and inside both, pillars and roofs
Carv'd work, the hand of fam'd Artificers
In Cedar, Marble, Ivory or Gold.
Thence to the gates cast round thine eye, and see
What conflux issuing forth, or entring in,
Pretors, Proconsuls to thir Provinces
Hasting or on return, in robes of State;
Lictors and rods the ensigns of thir power,
Legions and Cohorts, turmes of horse and
    wings;
Or Embassies from Regions far remote
In various habits on the *Appian* road,
Or on the *Aemilian*, some from farthest South,
Syene, and where the shadow both way falls,
Meroe Nilotic Isle, and more to West,
The Realm of Bocchus to the Black-moor Sea;
From the *Asian* Kings and *Parthian* among these,
From *India* and the golden *Chersoness*
And utmost *Indian* Isle *Taprobane*,
Dusk faces with white silken Turbants wreath'd:
From *Gallia*, *Gades* and the *British* West,
Germans and *Scythians*, and *Sarmatians* North
Beyond *Danubius* to the *Tauric* Pool.
All Nations now to *Rome* obedience pay,
To *Rome's* great Emperour, whose wide
    domain
In ample Territory, wealth and power,
Civility of Manners, Arts, and Arms,
And long Renown thou justly mays't prefer
Before the Parthian; these two Thrones except,
The rest are barbarous, and scarce worth the
    fight,
Shar'd among petty Kings too far remov'd.

The foregoing brief survey of Rome and her arts will have shown, it is hoped, what manner of city it was to which Paul came, and why it was essential for him to be there. If, in Paul's view, he was the messenger of a new dispensation to all the world, then he could only fulfil his mission by operating in and from that world's centre. This view is, not unnaturally, shared by St Luke. In writing *Acts* Luke had a double purpose. First he wanted to shew that the new Way was no threat to Roman rule, and that its great apostle had in fact always been on excellent terms with Roman representatives; secondly, he wanted to show Theophilus just how he, Luke, had come to be a Christian. The abrupt ending of *Acts* has puzzled many; but it is as though Luke were saying to his friend: 'Well, here is Paul at his journey's end: you know the rest.'

Before concluding this narrative, it may be well to point out not only how justified Paul's

Above, left:
The goddess Isis, the Egyptian deity who captured the imagination of the Romans and became a favourite with them. This statue is from Alexandria of the Roman period and little is to be seen of her true Egyptian character. However she is wearing the drapery at her breast and the knot of Isis – the *tat*, an early fertility symbol.

Right:
Sarapis, the pseudo-Egyptian god originated by Ptolemy Soter as a more suitable deity for his Greek subjects than those of his newly-acquired domain of Egypt. Sarapis, an amalgam of Zeus, Osiris and Dionysos, was a remarkably successful creation and very popular with the Romans, who often regarded him as the consort of Isis. He wears an emblem of fertility as a crown. Sculpture in the Capitoline Museum.

resolution had been proved, but how remarkably timely his advent was. That the Romans were not wholly insensitive to the immaterial is evident from their appreciation of both art and nature. But in the realm of the spirit they were by no means so happy. The old state religion, such as is referred to on the *Ara Pacis*, with its sacrifices, its formulae and its taboos, had long since ceased to provide any satisfaction to the Roman soul. It was a collection of dry-as-dust prohibitions and regulations, utterly without life. Indeed religion it could hardly be called any more. It was really little but a web of superstitions. The ordinary Roman was continually enveloped by a cloud of fear—fear of nature, of unseen powers, malignant and vindictive spirits. From this underworld of terror, his shadowy ancestral gods did nothing to release him: all too often they increased his anxiety. That is why we find in the Rome of Paul's day a hankering for *salus,* that is health, or salvation. The quest had begun long before. It had been satisfied from two sources. The first has already been mentioned. It was philosophy.

There is no doubt that for many elevated souls, philosophy did make a satisfying appeal. This was particularly true of Stoicism. But as already noted, the founder of Stoicism was a Semite. So close to

Judaism did Stoicism seem to be that Josephus, writing largely for Gentiles, can say that the Pharisees are the Stoics of Jewry. It is true also that much of the Stoic outlook did pass into Christianity, especially into its Puritan manifestations. But philosophy did not satisfy the spiritual needs of the ordinary man and woman. What did satisfy them were the mystery religions of the Orient. This is the cardinal fact that dominates the spiritual scene of Paul's day.

The first eastern deity to reach Rome was Cybele, the Great Mother, during the second Punic War. When in the year 205 BC the Sybilline books, the official encyclopaedia of magic, were consulted, they gave the amazing answer that if the Great Mother were brought to Rome, Hannibal would leave Italy. In the following April, she arrived, in the form of a black aerolith supplied by King Attalus I of Pergamum. The oracle of Delphi had favoured the idea, and so had the great Scipio himself. Cybele was given a flattering official reception, in which the patrician matrons of Rome played a leading rôle, and sure enough the very next year Hannibal left Italy, never to return.

Cybele was soon joined by her consort, Attis. He hailed originally from Thrace and his worship often involved orgiastic exhibitions which induced

frenzied 'possession' ending in self-castration. Such cults as these, because they were so un-Roman and because unlike the rites of Roman priestcraft, they allowed the worshippers to join in, made a wide appeal to souls in search of novel and potent spiritual tonics. It was to them that the word 'fanatic' was first applied. They appealed to the emotions rather than to reason. The death and resurrection of Attis was represented by a decorated tree, rather like our Christmas tree. The festival was commemorated hard by the imperial palace itself. The figure of Cybele was carried on a chariot which seems to prefigure the veneration paid to statues of Our Lady in the streets of Seville during Holy Week.

From Egypt came Isis and Sarapis. Isis enjoyed imperial patronage, and Sarapis became widely popular. (The best extant head of him came to light in London.) The Sarapeum in Hadrian's villa at Tibur is one of its most impressive precincts. Syrian deities gradually attained a pre-eminence, Astarte and Atargatis among them. Mithras, the Persian sun god, had thousands of votaries. A favourite with soldiers was Jupiter Dolichenus, who came from the Upper Euphrates. He is nowhere mentioned in any literary source, and yet more than a hundred inscriptions to him are known

from regions as far apart as Africa and Britain. Generally the Syrian deities were connected with the sun. There is only one sun, and so these cults, like the creed of the Stoics, were well on the way to monotheism.

The monotheists par excellence had for centuries been the Jews. During their captivity in the sixth century BC 'beyond the river', they had absorbed much Babylonian lore. So had the Syrians. In Cumont's words: 'Chaldean astrology, of which the Syrian priests were convinced disciples, had supplied them with the elements of a scientific theology. It had led them to the idea of a god enthroned far away from the earth, above the stars, almighty, universal and eternal, everything here below being regulated by the revolutions of the heavens during infinite cycles of years; and it had at the same time taught them to adore the sun, the radiant source of earthly life and human reason'.

Thus two parallel streams of monotheism were flowing from the east at the same time—the Jewish form based on the unique moral sanctions of the Law and the sublime admonitions of the Prophets, and the solar version.

What differentiated Judaism from all the other cults was that it insisted on moral sanctions, and that it demanded absolute obedience. All the other religions were optional—you simply chose the one you thought would give you the most *salus*. Morality came second, indeed into some it did not enter at all.

Christianity inherited the Jewish ethic. Of all the religions that flourished in Paul's day, Judaism and Christianity are the only two that flourish now. Paul's supreme, unique achievement is that it was he who, by making Rome his centre, gave the Judaeo-Christian ethic to the Roman world. He thus ensured that when the Rome of the Caesars disintegrated, it would be succeeded by that of Christ and his Saints.

Facing page:
Paul was beheaded, according to tradition, but there exists no certain proof of when or how he actually died. It was almost certainly during Nero's persecution. This representation of the event is a fifteenth-century relief from the Ciborium of Sixtus IV in the grotto of the Vatican Basilica.

Left:
The Church of St Paul without the Walls lies about a quarter of a mile from the Porta San Paolo, and it was on this spot that Paul was buried. The exterior of the church gives little idea of the magnificent interior: it is constructed after the manner of the early basilicas, and the first one on this site was dedicated during the reign of Valentinian II in 388 AD. The present church was built on the ruins of the old in 1854, after a disastrous fire.

EPILOGUE

Of Paul's last days we know no more than we do of his first. On arrival in the city he was allowed to live by himself, with a sentry to guard him (*Acts* XXVIII. 16). After three days he called the chief of the Jews together. He at once told them that despite what they had heard about him, he had done nothing inimical to Jewry or to its traditions and teaching. But here he was, a prisoner of the Romans. They would have let him go free, but because of Jewish accusations he had been 'constrained to appeal unto Caesar'. Not that he had anything to accuse his nation of. That is why he had asked the Jews to come and see him, because '. . . that for the hope of Israel I am bound with this chain'.

The Jewish elders were very tactful. At all costs they must avoid contention: after all it was only eleven years since Claudius had banished the whole community on account of their riotous divisions, and they were not going to risk that again. They assured him they had received no adverse report about him from Judaea, either in writing or orally. They would be glad to know what Paul thought, because—they had to admit it—the Christians were everywhere spoken against. Paul agreed to expound his faith to them, and a date was fixed for a hearing. Many of the Jewish community came to Paul's lodging, and he explained his view of salvation through Jesus and of the kingdom of God, basing his arguments on the Mosaic law and the Prophets. Some of his auditors accepted them, some did not: they could not agree. Paul warned them of the consequences of being deaf to his teaching, quoting the rebuke of *Isaiah* (VI. 9) to those who heard but would not understand, and saw but refused to perceive. The salvation of God, he added, was now sent to the Gentiles, and they would hear it.

The Jews went away, and presumably argued the whole question over among themselves.

Paul settled down to residence in Rome. It lasted two whole years during which he lived and preached confidently and without any interference in his own hired house, receiving all who came to him.

So ends *Acts*; for as has already been said, Luke's purpose in writing it was now accomplished.

Of Paul's subsequent history and end we really know almost nothing. That he intended to visit Spain we know, but not that he ever went there. The conjecture that he was released, and went on a journey which took him to Spain and to Greece and Crete, was then re-arrested, stood a second trial and perished in the Neronian persecution of AD 64, rests on no trustworthy evidence.

Leaving aside later, legendary, descriptions of Paul's death, in the so-called *Acts of Paul*, compiled at the end of the second century, the earliest testimony to his martyrdom, and a reliable one, comes in the letter of Bishop Clement of Rome to the Corinthians already cited.

'Let us set before our eyes the good apostles. Peter, who because of unrighteous jealousy suffered not one, nor two but many trials, and having given his testimony went to the glorious place which was his due. Because of jealousy and strife Paul shewed the way to win the prize of endurance. Seven times he was in bonds, he was driven away as an exile, he was a herald both in East and West, he won the noble glory of his faith. He taught righteousness to all the world, and when he had reached the limit of the West, he gave his testimony before rulers, and thus passed from the world and was taken up to the Holy Place, the greatest example of endurance.'

The phrase 'the limit of the West' has caused much dispute. In ordinary parlance it could easily mean Spain. But it need not: from the point of view of the Corinthians to whom Clement is writing the limit of the West for Paul, that is the most westerly point he ever reached, was Rome itself, where Clement was writing. The theory that Clement was merely echoing *Romans* xv. 24, in which Paul says he hopes to visit Spain, seems unnecessary and unconvincing.

We do not even know the year of Paul's death. Some would put it in 60, others in 64, others again as late as 67 or even 68. On the other hand the place of his execution is attested by an early and constant tradition. He was led out of the city through the Porta Trigemina, past the Pyramid of Cestius at the foot of which now lies the body of John Keats. The procession turned into the Ostian Way. Where the basilica of St Paul without the Walls now stands, they turned left and onto the Laurentian Way. At the third milestone they reached *Aquae Salviae*, the Salvian Marsh, where to-day is the Trappist monastery of *Tre Fontane*, Three Springs. The monastery is the oldest in Rome, the original church having been founded by Pope Honorius I (625–40). It lies in a little dell, adorned with trees and flowers, an oasis of silence amid the noise and clamour of life outside. There are three shrines within the precincts, one of which shelters the three fountains. It was built in 1599. The monastery was almost deserted for a time, but in 1868 it was made over to the French Trappists, who by planting eucalyptus trees reclaimed the marshy ground.

Unless there were tradition to support it no one would have suggested this out-of-the-way place as the site of Paul's execution. But as we learn from Tacitus (*History* IV. 11) execution outside the walls was a Roman custom. Here Paul was beheaded. His grave was nearer Rome, where the great Basilica was to arise.

In the third century the body of Paul, like that of Peter from the Vatican, appears to have been briefly removed for safety to the catacombs of St Sebastian on the Via Appia. This double preservation is celebrated in the feast of SS Peter and Paul on 29 June. The remains were afterwards replaced in their original burial places in the churches built by Constantine.

The basilica of St Paul without the Walls is now almost engulfed by the ever-encroaching suburbs of Rome. Hard by are the unheeding highways that lead to the airport and the seaside; but the church itself is set in a little park beneath a wooded knoll, and in spring it wears an almost gentle aspect.

The building was founded by the emperor Valentinian II in 388 on the site of a small church of Constantine's. It was a five-aisled apsidal basilica, the central nave being unroofed, and so reproduced almost exactly in style and dimensions the Forum of Trajan, which until the end of the world of pagan Rome was accounted the city's most majestic creation. The architrave was supported by eighty columns of pavonazzetto and Parian marble. It is now roofed. It is 130 yards long, 65 feet wide and 75 feet high. Over the centuries the church was embellished with frescoes and mosaics, and in the thirteenth century magnificent cloisters were added. These still survive, but the fabric of the basilica was wrecked by fire on the night of the 15–16 July 1823. Only the columns and the external walls remained of the accumulated work of fourteen centuries, the least changed and least restored of the great basilicas of Rome.

The church was rebuilt, but only after the demolition of much that might have been saved. The new basilica was consecrated in 1854. Mehmet Ali of Egypt contributed pillars of alabaster, Tsar Nicholas of Russia columns of malachite. Because the basilica was formerly under the protection of the sovereigns of England, the emblem of the Order of the Garter may still be discerned among the lavish decoration. The roof is now supported by eighty columns of granite from the Simplon.

To enter this pillared forest, dimly glowing in the half-light shed by the opaque alabaster windows in the side walls and clerestory, is to experience a sort of participation in the personality of Paul himself, its depths, its darknesses, its disasters, and its overcoming strength and triumph.

In this shrine ended the earthly Journeys of Saint Paul. His spiritual journeys know no end.

ACKNOWLEDGMENTS

Our knowledge of Saint Paul derives almost wholly from *The Acts of the Apostles*, and from the letters—the Epistles—of Paul himself. Of those attributed to him, I have followed Bornkamm in regarding the following as genuine: *1 Thessalonians* and *Galatians* the greater part of his *correspondence with Corinth, Philippians, Philemon* and *Romans*.

The remainder, *1 & 2 Timothy, Titus, Ephesians, Colossians, 2 Thessalonians,* Bornkamm classifies as 'Deutero-Pauline', that is as reflecting Pauline ideas, but in a later stage of Christian evolution.

For the background of Paul's ministry, other ancient writers are of value: Tacitus, Suetonius, Dio, Josephus, Pliny, Clement, Tertullian, each of whom is cited in his place.

Of modern writers on Paul, the company is very great. For the study of his journeys, with which this book is concerned, all research must be based on the works of Sir William Ramsay; *Pauline Studies, The Cities of St Paul, Luke the Physician, St Paul the Traveller and the Roman Citizen.* After a lapse of more than half a century, the work of Ramsay is still a beacon to guide and warn.

Dr T. R. Glover's *Paul of Tarsus* (1925) is an excellent exposition, for English readers, of Paul's complex personality and mission. *Paul of Tarsus* by Joseph Holzner is a translation of his *Paulus, sein Leben unde seine Briefe*. It appeared in 1944 and is specially useful in giving the Jewish background of Paul. All episodes connected with Palestine and Jerusalem are lucidly and precisely set out in Abel's *Histoire de la Palestine depuis la conquête d'Alexandre jusqu'à l'Invasion Arabe,* (Vol I) 1952. For the history of the Church in general there is no better authority than the monumental *Histoire de L'Eglise* of Lebreton & Zeiller (Fliche et Martin, still in course of publication).

The modern analyses of Paul and his work that I have found most helpful are *Paolo Apostolo,* by Guiseppe Ricciotti (4th edition, 1951) which contains a splendidly detailed and documented gazeteer, with illustrations; and *Paul* by Günther Bornkamm (German edition 1969; English 1971).

As so often before, I have received unstinted help from my friend The Rev Joseph Crehan, SJ, of London. In Malta, my work has been generously forwarded by H. L. Monsignor Gerarda, Bishop Co-adjutor of Malta, the Rev Vito Borgia, of the Church of Our Lady of Damascus, Valetta, and Dr Hugh Schonfield. I thank them all.

Professor Lloyd and the Royal Central Asian Society have most kindly allowed me to quote from the lecture on Early Travellers in Asia Minor which he delivered before the Royal Central Asian Society when receiving their Gold Medal in 1971, and which was published in *Asian Affairs* in June 1972.

I have made no attempt to supply a definitive chronological table: every important date is widely disputed. Instead, I have tried to take each event as it comes, and to give the various dates suggested for it.

Parts of this book have appeared in other forms in publications issued by Messrs Hamlyn, Messrs Hodder & Stoughton and the *Nursing Mirror and Midwives' Gazette*. I am grateful to all of them for permission to use this material.

S.P.

Black and white photographs
Alinari, Florence 17, 47, 96, 104–105, 126–127; Alinari-Giraudon 74 left; Barnaby's Picture Library, London 74 right; Barnaby's-S. B. Davie 86–87; Barnaby's-Peter Larsen 37 bottom; Barnaby's-Josip Ciganovic Omcikus 129; Bayerische Staatsgemaldesammlungen, Munich 75; British Museum 40 bottom; J. Allan Cash Ltd., London 73, 95, 119, 125, 139; Daily Telegraph Colour Library, London 76; Paul Demajo 120; Arpad Elfer, London 70–71; Werner Forman 91 left, 91 right; Hachette, Paris 83; Sonia Halliday 32 left; Hamlyn Group Picture Library 49 left; Israel Department of Antiquities and Museums 13; A. F. Kersting, London 16 left, 16 right, 44–45 top, 44–45 bottom, 73 top, 94; Lauros-Giraudon 68–69; Mansell Collection, London 11, 20 left, 42–43, 71; Mansell-Alinari 11, 14–15, 34, 38 top right, 38 bottom, 78, 86, 132–133, 138; Mansell-Anderson 33, 38 top left, 39, 61, 64, 109, 116, 134 top, 137 left; Middle East Archive 9, 24–25, 28–29, 32 right, 35, 45 bottom; Antonello Perissinotto, Padua 112, 134 bottom, 137 right; Picturepoint Ltd., London 50, 52, 65, 70 bottom, 88–89 bottom, 93, 116 right; Popperfoto, London 20 right, 51, 66, 97, 114–115, 130; Popperfoto-Donald McLeish Collection 90; Radio Times Hulton Picture Library 40 top, 48, 58–59, 121, 131; George Rodger-Magnum 10–11; Scala, Florence 49 right; Spectrum Colour Library, London 37 top, 53; Edwin Smith 81, 127, 128; Turkish Tourist Office, London 85 top; Roger-Viollet, Paris 56–57, 63, 117, 123; Z.E.F.A., Düsseldorf 55, 82, 84, 85 bottom, 88–89 top, 122.

Colour photographs
J. Allan Cash Ltd. 102–103, 102 bottom; A. F. Kersting, London 30 bottom, 98 bottom; Magnum 22 bottom, 26 bottom; Middle East Archive 26–27, 27 bottom, 30 top, 103 bottom; Picturepoint Ltd. 23, 98 top, 111 top; Scala, Florence 19; Spectrum Colour Library 27 top, 110 bottom; University Library, Cambridge 98 top; Roger Wood, London 99, 106 bottom; Z.E.F.A., Düsseldorf 22 top, 106 top, 107, 110 top, 111 bottom.

INDEX

Figures in *italics* refer to captions

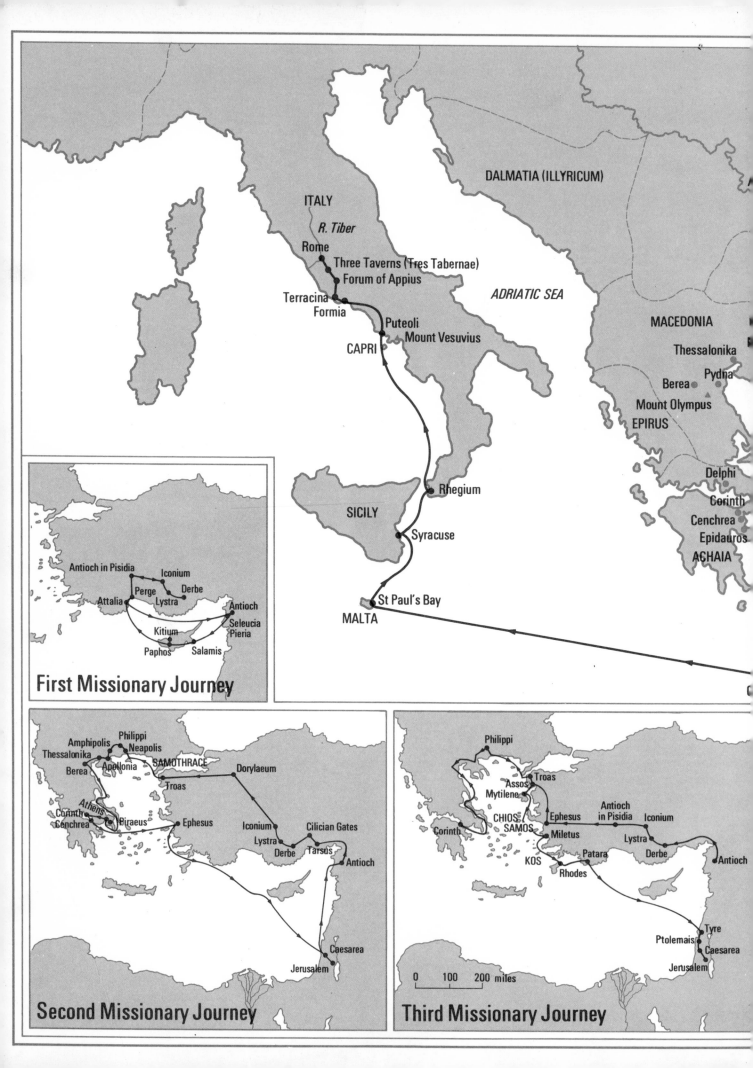

ITALY

R. Tiber

Rome

Three Taverns (Tres Tabernae)

Forum of Appius

Terracina
Formia

Puteoli

Mount Vesuvius

CAPRI

DALMATIA (ILLYRICUM)

ADRIATIC SEA

MACEDONIA

Thessalonika

Pydna

Berea

Mount Olympus

EPIRUS

Delphi

Corinth

Cenchrea

Epidauros

ACHAIA

Rhegium

SICILY

Syracuse

St Paul's Bay

MALTA

First Missionary Journey

Antioch in Pisidia

Iconium

Perge

Derbe

Attalia

Lystra

Antioch

Kitium

Seleucia
Pieria

Paphos

Salamis

Second Missionary Journey

Amphipolis

Philippi

Thessalonika

Neapolis

Apollonia

SAMOTHRACE

Berea

Dorylaeum

Athens

Troas

Corinth

Piraeus

Ephesus

Cenchrea

Iconium

Cilician Gates

Lystra

Derbe

Tarsus

Antioch

Caesarea

Jerusalem

Third Missionary Journey

Philippi

Assos

Troas

Mytilene

CHIOS

Ephesus

Antioch
in Pisidia

Iconium

SAMOS

Corinth

Miletus

Lystra

KOS

Patara

Derbe

Antioch

Rhodes

Tyre

Ptolemais

Caesarea

Jerusalem

0   100   200 miles

THE JOURNEYS OF StPAUL

THE JOURNE
StPAU

STEWART

HAMLYN   LONDON·NEW